JEREMY

MURDER
ON
ELM STREET

A TRUE-LIFE CRIME STORY

BEAVER'S POND
PRESS

Murder on Elm Street © 2024 by Jeremy L. Luberts

The interview and audio transcripts included in this book are part of the public record.

Beaver's Pond Press is committed to turning interesting people into independent authors. In that spirit, we are proud to offer this book to our readers; however, the story, the experiences, and the words are the author's alone.

Cover image and author photo provided by the author
Book design and typesetting by Dan Pitts

ISBN 13: 978-1-64343-597-8
Library of Congress Catalog Number: 2023911541
Printed in the United States of America
First Edition 2024
27 26 25 24 23   5 4 3 2 1

BEAVER'S POND
PRESS

939 West Seventh Street
Saint Paul, MN 55102
(952) 829-8818
www.BeaversPondPress.com

Contact the author at murderonelmstreet@gmail.com for speaking engagements and interviews.

To the memory of Washington County Attorney
Peter Orput.

Orput set his life aside to help the residents
of Morrison County,

and his generosity will never be forgotten.

CONTENTS

Chapter 1: The Call. 1

Chapter 2: Responding to the Residence 5

Chapter 3: Making Contact. 7

Chapter 4: The Shocking Discovery. 12

Chapter 5: Preserving the Scene. 17

Chapter 6: Back at the Office 22

Chapter 7: The Interview. 29

Chapter 8: The Second Interview. 81

Chapter 9: Search Warrants and Identity
of the Teenagers 86

Chapter 10: The Third and Final Interview 94

Chapter 11: Back Home. 117

Chapter 12: Search Warrants of the Vehicles 122

Chapter 13: Tragedy at Home. 128

Chapter 14: The First Court Appearance 136

Chapter 15: Identical Twin Deputies. 149

Chapter 16: Continuing the Investigation 155

Chapter 17: Coming Home. 162

Chapter 18: Others Involved. 166

Chapter 19: Another Search Warrant at
Smith's Residence 175

Chapter 20: A Good Idea 179

Chapter 21: Amazing Discovery 182

Chapter 22: Bail Hearing. 189

Chapter 23: Autopsy Reports 194

Chapter 24: Divided Community 200

Chapter 25: Washington County Attorney. 203

Chapter 26: Grand Jury Hearing 206

Chapter 27: Strange Activity. 214

Chapter 28: Omnibus Hearing. 217

Chapter 29: The Castle Doctrine 224

Chapter 30: Moving Out 227

Chapter 31: The Jury Trial, Day 1. 231

Chapter 32: Jury Trial, Day 2 & 3. 238

Chapter 33: Jury Trial, Day 4 & 5. 243

Chapter 34: Jury Trial, Day 6 249

Chapter 35: Jury Trial, Day 7, "The Verdict" 252

Chapter 36: Post-Conviction News Coverage 264

Chapter 37: Conclusion. 267

THE CALL

On November 23, 2012, the temperature outside was twenty-eight degrees. There was a light wind out of the south and a couple of inches of fresh snow on the ground, which was normal for that time of year. I was born, grew up, and continue to live in the small town of Little Falls, Minnesota. Our population is 8,300 people. Little Falls is the childhood home of Charles Lindbergh and the county seat of Morrison County.

The Mississippi River runs through our small town dividing the east side from the west. The river also divides our county roughly in half. Residents of Morrison County enjoy four distinct seasons. Abundant fields, woods, lakes, and rivers offer plenty of outdoor activities for people to enjoy year-round.

I'm Sergeant Investigator Jeremy Luberts. I was a deputy sheriff for fifteen years and a sergeant investigator with the Morrison County Sheriff's Office for over two years by the time our story began. It was 1:00 p.m., and I was enjoying my day off. My wife Chrissy, my nine-year-old daughter Hailey, and I were sharing a big blanket, snuggling up together on the couch watching Disney's *The Santa Clause.*

I love the holiday season. In our house, we put our Christmas tree up and string the outside lights a week after Halloween. That year, I had managed not to turn the lights on until November 22, just in time for Thanksgiving. I waited that long not because I wanted to, but because I didn't want the neighbors to think I was weird. The guys at work, on the other hand, were already familiar with my extreme enthusiasm for the holidays; I'd been listening to Christmas music in my squad car since early October.

Chrissy and I both worked Thanksgiving Day. I worked the day shift, following up on investigations of recent burglaries, reviewing complaints, and going over reports other deputies had made on cases that were headed to the county attorney for possible criminal charges. I also did some patrolling in the county. There was not much call activity, so I had a fairly quiet day for a change.

Chrissy worked the afternoon shift at the St. Cloud Hospital ER where she is a registered nurse. Her night consisted of dealing with drunks and prescription-narcotic seekers. We both had our hands full working for and with the public. We got into these jobs because we like helping people, but many days, there is no pleasing anyone, no matter how hard you try. Some people won't be happy until others are miserable too. As the old saying goes, misery loves company.

That day was going to be our day to relax and not deal with the public. We were both looking forward to having the next three days off together.

My cell phone rang. The department had only two investigators—my partner, Sergeant Investigator Jason Worlie, and myself. As such, we were both effectively on call twenty-four hours a day, seven days a week. Work had called me multiple times before, often while I was out with my family. Sometimes, someone just had a question regarding a case. Other times, they needed me to come in. These interruptions to our family life had started getting to Chrissy.

Immediately, Chrissy gave me a look. It was the kind of look that freezes your soul, that would kill you, if looks could kill. I have a strong suspicion that Eve was first to give this look to Adam after eating the forbidden fruit and becoming conscious of them both being naked. After everything I've seen in my career, I don't scare easily. Yet, to this day, this look from Chrissy bothers me.

My caller ID showed it was Deputy David Scherping calling. I answered the phone, hoping to keep things brief. "Hello Dave, what's up?"

He told me he had just talked with a complainant named William Anderson. William lived on Elm Street, just north of town in the Belle Prairie Township. William told Dave that his neighbor, Byron Smith, called him that morning looking for a suggestion for a local attorney. He said Byron had been having problems with people breaking into his home. He suspected that someone had recently broken into Byron's house, and he thought Byron might have shot the intruder.

It is not uncommon for us to get calls from people who exaggerate things, and this call seemed to fit that category. Yet, for some reason I couldn't explain, I got a strange feeling that there might be something more to this call. Something was telling me I needed to follow up on this further. I decided I had better go in and investigate.

"Dave, this sounds suspicious. I'm going to get ready, and I'll meet you at the office. We'll go over to the Smith residence together." Dave thanked me for being willing to come in and give him a hand.

I hung up the phone and told Chrissy I had to go into work. That went over like a fart in church—the kind that's so loud, even the Father is inclined to interrupt his sermon to comment, "Someone is windy out there today." I had done that when I was nine. I was sitting in the back of the church, the old stained wooden bench beneath my butt cheeks. I thought it was pretty funny at the time. Grandma was laughing so hard she had tears in her eyes. But Grandpa, who was seated two people down from me, was so angry that he grabbed me one-handed, and with a mighty jerk, I flew through the air and landed next to him. He didn't have to say a word. Everyone's eyes were on me, and I knew at that moment that I had done something I should not have. Chrissy wore the same angry expression my grandpa had when I told her I had to go into work.

She wasn't feeling the greatest to begin with and wanted me to take care of her that day, to massage her head and feet, make supper, and just be there for her. She told me she was feeling weak, and she looked pale. I felt like shit about leaving, but I also felt I had no choice.

I went upstairs and changed into my uniform. It took me about ten minutes to get my pants, shirt, bulletproof vest, duty belt, and boots on. I opened the door to leave, telling Chrissy, "Love you, be back soon." I logged into my computer while I waited for my Chevy Tahoe to warm up. I radioed the dispatcher, "106, 800, I'll be in service," then drove five blocks to the sheriff's office. 106 was my badge number, and 800 is the dispatch's call number.

RESPONDING TO THE RESIDENCE

I arrived at the sheriff's office at 1:23 p.m. I met with Deputy Scherping and Deputy Rick Mattison. I decided the three of us would respond to the call about Byron Smith's residence together. Elm Street, where Byron lived, was about a five-minute drive from our office. As a sergeant, it was my job to decide how we'd approach these situations.

"Dave, you and I will drive up to the house and make contact with Smith. Rick, you follow behind us, stay back, and remain nearby in case something happens so that you can get us help." We didn't know what was going on at the residence, and my philosophy was always to be safe rather than sorry. Walking into an unknown situation is always risky.

The three of us each got into our squad cars and drove to the residence. I was the lead vehicle, Dave was behind me, and Rick brought up the rear. I took 4th Street N.E to Haven Road, where I turned right. From Haven Road, I turned left onto Riverwood Drive and drove a short distance to Elm Street. I then took a left turn onto Elm Street. The road continues for about a quarter mile before it dead-ends at Byron Smith's driveway.

As I was approaching, Bill (or William Anderson) was walking down his driveway to meet me. Bill lived two doors down from Byron Smith. I stopped, rolled down my window, and talked with him. Byron had called him multiple times that morning asking him for assistance in locating an attorney. Bill told me that Byron had been having problems with people breaking into his house.

I specifically asked Bill, "Did Byron tell you if he shot anyone?"

Bill told me, "No, Byron didn't tell me that."

That made me feel a little bit better. After talking with Bill, I drove to Smith's house. We arrived at his residence at 1:34 p.m. His rambler-style brick home was at the end of a long dirt driveway. I parked in front of the attached garage and Dave parked next to me. There were no vehicles parked outside.

I radioed my dispatcher, "106, 800, 109 and I will be out at the residence."

MAKING CONTACT

Dave and I exited our squad cars in unison and started walking to the front door. An older male wearing a blue-jean jacket and jeans that looked as though he'd slept in them came out of the house with his hands raised above his messy gray hair. I realized this wasn't going to be our typical nuisance call.

"Are you Byron Smith?" I asked.

"Yes," he answered.

I tried to approach the situation with kindness and understanding. I needed to get as much information from him as I could, and to do that, I had to gain his trust so he would talk with me. I badly needed to figure out what the hell was going on. It's not every day that someone walks out of their house to meet you with their hands raised above their head.

I had to think fast about what to do. I told Byron, "I heard something might have happened at your residence recently. Would it be okay if we came inside and talked with you?" Byron put his hands down, opened the door, and invited us into his house.

We entered between the laundry room area to our right and the kitchen to our left. In front of us was a long hallway that led to bedrooms, a bathroom, and the living room. Just off the kitchen there was a stairwell that led to a basement. Byron asked us to follow him down the hallway and told us, "There's something I need to show you in my bedroom."

We followed Byron to the end of the hallway. Byron opened his bedroom door. It was cold in the room, and I could see that a window had been broken. There was broken glass lying on a desk below the window and on the floor. The broken glass inside the bedroom indicated that someone had broken the window from the outside. I asked Byron what happened, and he said, "Someone broke into my house yesterday."

I asked him if he knew how it happened, and he said, "I think someone used their elbow to break the window, then crawled in." The window was made from old thin glass, and it appeared possible that someone could have broken it just by hitting the window with their elbow.

Thinking this was going to be another burglary report, I breathed a little sigh of relief. Byron then asked us to follow him down the hallway back to the kitchen. Byron told us that initially, he could hear somebody trying the doorknob to his house on the door off the kitchen area. He heard somebody walking around outside on his deck. Byron said a short time later, he heard the glass break in the bedroom and then heard footsteps coming down the hallway from the bedroom. Byron told us he was in the basement of the house when he heard all this.

Byron seemed a little nervous, but he kept calm. He looked at me and said, "There's something I need to show you in the basement."

I followed Byron down the stairs, and Dave was behind me. As I stepped down, I could see what appeared to be blood on a rug at the bottom of the stairs. There was also a possible blood stain on the wall. The small hairs on the back of my neck stood on end. I looked back at Dave and whispered to him, "Turn your recorder on."

Our patrol deputies all have digital recorders in their squad cars and carry a pocket microphone that records audio. Thank goodness Dave was with me, because our department didn't give investigators these recorders in our squad cars. I was told it was because of budget issues. I found out later that my lack of recorder didn't matter because the dang thing hadn't picked up any audio in the basement of the house anyways. Still, to tape our interactions with Byron was a good idea at the time.

When we got to the bottom of the stairs, Byron pointed to a chair that was just to the left of the stairwell. The chair appeared to be a La-Z-Boy type, brownish-red in color. The odd thing about the chair was its placement. I noticed that it was surrounded by bookshelves so the only view a person would have while sitting in that chair would be of the stairwell. I also noticed a pair of tennis shoes underneath the chair. Byron looked at me and said, "I had been sitting in that chair reading a book when a person broke into my house."

Byron then told me, "After I heard the window break upstairs, I then heard footsteps coming down the hallway. Then I heard the footsteps start coming down the stairwell." He told me, "As the male party got down the stairwell to where I could see his hips, I opened fire with my Mini-14 rifle. I had it loaded and sitting next to me. The male party fell down the stairs after being shot and landed at the bottom of the steps. I then walked over to the male party and shot him until he was dead."

I stood there in complete silence, somewhat shocked after what he had just told me. I looked over at Dave and he had a "holy shit" look on his face, the same look I'm pretty sure I had on mine. And we'd learn, this was just the beginning.

Byron then looked at us and said, "After shooting the male party, I grabbed a small tarp and placed the body on the tarp and moved the body from the bottom of the stairwell to a separate room in my office work area."

I thought to myself, *Why the hell would you do something like that?*

"After moving the body, I went and sat back down in my chair near the stairwell. A short time later, I heard some more footsteps walking down the hallway. I then heard footsteps coming down the stairwell, and as the person was coming down the stairs, I shot her. After shooting her, she fell down the stairs to the floor. I went over to shoot her again with the Mini-14 rifle, and my gun jammed. She looked at me and kind of smirked or laughed. I then took my .22 revolver I had on my waist and shot her in the chest, aiming for her heart. After shooting her, I moved her body from the bottom of the steps back into my office work area and laid her next to the male party. I noticed that she was still breathing and gasping for breath, so I took my revolver and placed it under her chin and pulled the trigger to finish her off. I can't stand to see any animal or people suffer."

While Byron was telling me about his humanitarian practices, he put his right hand in the shape of a gun and placed his finger that was the barrel of the gun under his chin in the location where he told me he shot her. I thought to myself, *What kind of sick, twisted person does something like that? Let alone stand there with a relative calm about himself as he tells me this?*

I was working hard to keep my composure when I asked Byron, "When did this happen?"

Byron said, "This happened around noon yesterday, on Thanksgiving Day."

"Why didn't you report this incident to law enforcement yesterday?" I asked him.

"I didn't want to take you away from your families or bother you on Thanksgiving."

I thought to myself, *Really, are you kidding me? No one ever gives a shit about bothering us or calling us regarding any little thing that bothers them, especially on holidays. In fact, I wished he had called yesterday, because then, I was working. This was my day off, and it was always hard on my family when I had to give up our time off.*

At this point, though I'd seen blood stains, I hadn't seen any bodies, so I was still desperately holding onto hope that his whole crazy story wasn't real.

Byron then asked us to follow him back into his office work area. He led us through a door that was to the right at the bottom of his stairs. From that room, there was another closed door to our left.

"That's my office work area. The bodies are behind this door," he said.

My hands were shaking as I reached for the doorknob. I turned the knob slowly and opened the door, and there, my worst fears were realized.

THE SHOCKING DISCOVERY

Two bodies partially wrapped in a green camouflage tarp lay next to each other on the floor. They appeared to be young, a male and female, both in their teens. The female was wearing a black hooded sweatshirt that said "Hard Candy" on the front. She had the hood up around her head and the front was drawn tight against her face so all I could see was her eyes, nose, and mouth. She'd been trying to hide her face, likely from surveillance cameras. It looked like she had been in extreme pain when she took her last breaths. There was so much pain, it had remained frozen on her face after she passed.

There was a hole in her sweatshirt over the left arm. Through it, I could clearly see that a bullet had struck her left bicep, causing massive muscle tissue and bone damage. I have seen enough gunshot wounds in my career to know that she was probably shot by a high-powered rifle.

She was wearing black gloves on her hands, which I'm sure was to prevent her from leaving any fingerprints at the scene.

She had on blue jeans and gray boots.

Her sweatshirt was lifted in the front to just under her breasts. Her stomach was exposed. There was blood on her stomach and a small hole in her sweatshirt in her chest area. I lifted the sweatshirt and saw a smaller bullet hole in her chest. This wound had been bleeding out. This bullet hole appeared to have been caused by a small-caliber handgun. I knew this based on the size of the bullet hole and the lack of impact-force tissue damage present at its point of entry.

This young girl had been shot multiple times with two different guns. I couldn't help but think of my little girl at home that very moment, then of this girl's parents, who were out there somewhere, wondering where their daughter was or what she was doing. It hurt knowing that the parents of this young lady would never see their daughter alive again. A great sadness and anger came over me. I was sad because of what this girl's parents would have to go through. I was angry because the man who did this to her was standing right behind me acting like some kind of humanitarian because he had ended her life as he would an animal, referencing how he always puts a suffering creature out of its misery.

The young male was wearing a brown camouflage coat and blue jeans. He was not wearing any shoes, and I'm sure the tennis shoes I saw under the chair in the other room belonged to him.

His upper body and face were hidden underneath the tarp. I lifted the tarp to take a closer look. What I saw next was very disturbing. The boy had been shot in the head near his right eye with what appeared to be a high-power rifle. There was extensive muscle, bone, and tissue damage to his head. It was so extensive, I could see pieces of his brain. I put the tarp back down over his head so that I didn't have to look at him anymore.

The sight of these two young teenagers is forever burned into my memory. I will live with their faces and the details of this day for the rest of my life. I have a filing cabinet in my mind where I try to file and lock away all the bad stuff I have witnessed and experienced in my career, but there are some memories a person cannot forget. My filing cabinet is getting pretty full after seventeen years of seeing adults, children, and even infants killed in accidents, suicides, homicides, and natural deaths. All I can do is try to manage these memories, and hope they never come back to haunt me.

I asked Byron if there were any weapons the male or female party had on them when they broke in and he said, "I didn't see or notice any weapons on them."

I examined Byron more closely while he spoke. The clothing he was wearing appeared to have blood stains. I saw them on his shoes and his blue-jean jacket.

I then asked Byron to accompany me to the room nearer the stairwell, away from the deceased. I had to decide my next course of action. I knew Byron had the right to defend himself in his own home, especially since they'd broken in. I also know he had the right to use deadly force to protect himself.

The problem with what I saw was that these teens were not carrying any weapons, they were shot and killed over twenty-four hours before we arrived, and Byron never called law enforcement to report what happened—his neighbor did. He also admitted to me that after he shot the boy, and the boy was lying at the bottom of his stairs wounded, he basically executed him by shooting him in the head. At that point, the boy no longer posed a threat to him. Then after the boy was dead, Byron wrapped him in a tarp and dragged him off into another room.

To top things off, he told me he'd shot the girl while she was lying wounded at the bottom of the stairs. She was clearly no longer a threat. The girl laughed at him, he'd said, so he shot her multiple times. He told me he also dragged her body off into a different room and laid her next to the boy. Then, he said that because the female was still breathing, he gave her "a good clean finishing shot."

Byron's duty was to call law enforcement right away to report this incident. Then, to the best of his abilities, he should have administered first aid to the wounded, not executed them for his own self-gratification.

In a nice, understanding way, I told Byron, "Because of what happened here and because you were involved in a shooting, I have no choice but to place you under arrest and bring you to the sheriff's office."

Byron looked at me and said, "I understand, and I know that you are just doing your job."

I radioed my dispatcher "106, 800, I'll be 10-15," which means Byron was placed under arrest at approximately 1:43 p.m.

I told Dave to place handcuffs on Byron. He did so, and then we did a pat down search of Byron's clothing. We do a pat down search with every arrest to make sure the individual is not carrying any weapons that they could use in transit to the sheriff's office.

In Byron's right front pants pocket I found four shells for a rifle. I asked Byron if these were the shells for the Mini-14 rifle he used in the shootings and he said, "Yes, they are." In his left front pants pocket, I found four shells for the .22 caliber pistol. I asked Byron if these were the shells for the

.22 pistol he used in the shooting and he told me, "Yes they are for my .22 revolver pistol that I was carrying and used."

I placed the shells I found in his pants pockets on a small coffee table behind me. We then finished the pat down search of Byron, and did not find any other items on his person.

"Can you tell me again what type of guns you used in the shooting?" I asked Byron.

"A Mini-14 Ruger-brand rifle, and a .22 caliber nine-shot revolver pistol."

I asked him where the guns were currently located and he said, "I placed them in the upstairs closet near the entry door by the stairwell." I needed to know where the guns were for Dave's and my safety. Furthermore, they were key pieces of evidence in this case.

Dave and I then walked Byron upstairs. When we got to the entry door that is just off the stairwell, Byron told me, "The guns are in the two closets to our left. The .22 revolver is on the top shelf in the first closet and the Mini-14 rifle is leaning up against the wall in the second closet."

The closets are next to each other, and both doors were closed. I opened the doors and confirmed both guns were inside, in the locations where Byron told us they would be.

I then radioed Deputy Mattison to come to our location. We walked Byron outside and placed him in the back of Dave's squad car.

PRESERVING THE SCENE

Dave and Rick stood outside, waiting for next steps. Byron was secured in the back seat of Dave's squad car. I called my boss, Sheriff Michel Wetzel, and told him about everything I discovered and had done up to that point. He told me he would come to the scene so I could brief him on what I had. It is our department policy that the sheriff be notified of any deaths that occur in the county.

I then radioed my dispatch to contact the Minnesota Bureau of Criminal Apprehension to respond to the scene. The BCA is a statewide law enforcement agency that specializes in assisting other state and local law enforcement agencies with felony-level crimes including homicides, missing juveniles, missing adults, sex trafficking, drug sale, and drug-possession cases. The BCA has a mobile crime lab and agents who respond to crime scenes; map the scene; preserve and collect evidence such as DNA, fingerprints, tire and shoe impressions, and blood spatter; and collect and preserve electronic devices such as cell phones, computers, and surveillance-recording devices. They also collect and preserve firearms and bullets recovered from the scene, including those found in the bodies of the victims. They have the labs and the technicians to process all this evidence, and their experts can testify to what was discovered and what it all means.

Their agents assist with locating suspects, interviewing suspects and victims, obtaining search warrants, and following up as needed in these cases. The BCA does not come and take over the crime scene or the investigation. They are there to assist the law enforcement agency who is overseeing the case. Since I was the lead investigator in this case, I worked hand in hand with them.

I had worked with the BCA on previous homicide and officer-involved shooting cases in the county. They are a good group of people to work with. It usually takes them a couple of hours to get everything together and arrive at our crime scenes. There was plenty for me to do prior to their arrival.

I went to my squad car and retrieved my camera. I then obtained photographs of the outside and inside of the residence. When photographing a crime scene, I always started from the outside of the scene and worked my way in. That way, there was less chance I'd miss something. My goal, with photographing a scene, was to paint a picture for others to be able to see what happened. As the old saying goes, a picture is worth a thousand words. I truly believe this adage and have seen many court trials throughout the years where jury members respond to and appreciate officers who took the time to take good photographs. Doing so allows jury members to put themselves in the officer's shoes and see what they saw.

While looking around the outside of the house, I noticed Byron had surveillance cameras mounted in different locations. I saw cameras that faced the driveway, the upstairs entry door, the upper deck on the backside of the house, and the south entry door below the deck on the lower back of the house. I took pictures of all of them, hoping they were real, hooked-up, working cameras, and that they'd been recording at the time the break-in and shootings took place.

I took pictures of the broken window on the west side of the house. That was clearly the entry point the teens had used. The window belonged to Byron's bedroom. It appeared to me that they picked that particular window because that part of the house was surrounded by trees, and there was no surveillance camera on that side of the house. There is also no view of that side of the house from the roadway nor from any other residences.

Inside the house, I started upstairs and took pictures of all the rooms, but I paid close attention to key areas of interest, including Byron's bedroom with the broken window and the laundry room closets where he'd put the firearms he'd used in the shooting.

Then I moved to the stairwell. On my descent to the basement, I focused on the blood on the rug at the bottom of the stairs and the spot of blood on the wall at the bottom of the stairwell.

I then obtained pictures of the shells that I took out of Byron's pants pockets and placed on the coffee table. I photographed the La-Z-Boy chair Byron said he was sitting in, the tennis shoes under the chair, some energy bars and water bottles near the chair, and the bookshelves surrounding the chair. The energy bars and water bottles suggested that Byron was planning to spend a lot of time in that chair.

Tucked back in a corner, on the floor to the right of the chair, I saw a pair of jeans with what appeared to be blood on them. I took a picture of those jeans; they were puzzling to me. Why would there be a pair of jeans with blood on them lying in the corner of the basement? Who did they belong to? Was there another victim? I sure hoped not!

The basement entry door was made of wood. It had been patched with another piece of wood, as though someone had broken in before, and Byron or someone else had fixed it.

The last room I photographed was the back-office workroom where the bodies lay. It was not a sight I wanted to view again, but it had to be done. While I was standing there taking pictures of the victims, the distinct odor of human dead hit my nose like a ton of bricks. Immediately my stomach turned. I have smelled this foul odor many times in my career. Once you smell such an odor, you will never forget it. It is unmistakable. I have even tasted this odor hours and days after leaving a death scene. It has appeared while eating my breakfast, lunch, or supper. The odor sticks in your body for days and sometimes weeks after. I've inadvertently lost weight during these periods as I struggle to eat until the odor finally dissipates.

I feel sorry for anyone who goes into a bathroom after me if I've been at a death scene. A few times at work, I've heard the bathroom door open and hurried footsteps retreating shortly thereafter. That poor person just got a small sense of what it's like to be around a decomposing body. My family can attest to this.

On a table in the back of the room, I saw a TV monitor and digital video recorder. It appeared to be for the outside surveillance cameras. I was hopeful we'd be able to obtain a video recording for evidence.

After photographing the scene, I walked outside and met with Sheriff Wetzel. He was just arriving at the residence. I explained everything that happened up to that point. We decided to transport Byron to the sheriff's office so that we could attempt to obtain a statement from him. Dave transported Byron, and I told Rick to stay outside at the residence to secure the scene.

"Rick, no one is allowed to enter the house, including yourself, until we arrive back at the residence with a search warrant."

"I understand," Rick said.

Sheriff Wetzel, Dave, and I left the residence, and I followed Dave back to the office.

CHAPTER
6

BACK AT THE OFFICE

"Bring Byron into the interview room while I meet with Sheriff Wetzel in his office," I told Dave. In Michel's office, I told him that I was going to try to obtain a statement from Byron.

"Do you think that's a good idea or should we wait for the BCA to get here and attempt the statement then?" he asked.

I told him I should be the one to get a statement from Byron. "I built up a rapport with him at the scene, and if Byron's going to be willing to talk with anyone, it will probably be me."

I could see Michel had his doubts about letting me obtain the statement, but I was adamant. I needed to be the one to attempt to get that statement from him.

Michel told me to give him a few minutes and he'd let me know. I walked out of his office, and he shut the door behind me.

I sat down in my office for a little break. I was stewing and pretty pissed off that Michel was even considering allowing someone other than me to attempt the statement with Byron. I knew I had only two years' experience as an investigator, but I also had fifteen years under my belt as a patrol officer. I had interviewed many suspects involved in all kinds of crimes: sexual assaults, burglaries, domestic assaults, fraud, damage to property, arson, drug cases, and others. I had been very successful at getting confessions from people, and I had never had a statement thrown out of court because of improper procedure. In my seventeen years as an officer, I had not lost a single case in court.

I had interviewed a suspect involved in an attempted-murder case, but I had never interviewed a suspect involved in murder, let alone a double-murder case like this one.

Interviewing is a learned art. I have taken multiple unique training classes on how to interview a suspect. Training classes are fine for giving people new ideas for how to interview their subject, and the classes do teach proper procedure, but the classes cannot compare to real-world experience. The more interviews a person does in their career, the better they get at it. I wanted the experience of interviewing a murder suspect.

The best interview training I ever received came from being partnered with older deputies and investigators, those who had been in the department for 20 years or more. I took a little bit of knowledge from each one of them and added that to my own years of experience. Those experiences inform my personal interviewing style. I believe interviewing suspects is an art form, and I'm happy to say my interviewing skills haven't failed me yet.

I like to be up-front and honest with everyone I deal with. I'm not going to interview a person by telling them a bunch of lies to get them to talk with me. I don't believe in giving someone false hope. I don't play down the severity of someone's crime nor tell them that they won't go to jail or prison when there is a strong likelihood that they will.

If they ask, "Am I going to go to jail for this?" and the crime warrants that outcome, my answer will be *yes*. Then I'll offer a good explanation of that answer. I have witnessed far too many officers lie to suspects by saying *no*, or by pussyfooting around the question instead of giving the person a direct answer. I have more respect for people than that and won't do that to them.

The best way to piss someone off is to lie to them. They will find out, and the chances are high that the officer who lied will have to deal with that person again in the future. Good luck getting any cooperation from them at that later time if they know the officer lied to them before. And believe me, they will never forget what that officer did to them. Never!

I have arrested and interviewed many suspects who have told me about officers they despise because the person lied to them. In their eyes, that officer is now "lower than dogshit." (Their words, not mine.) Often, these individuals harbor hatred for all law enforcement officers after they've had negative dealings with just one. Then I have to work harder to get them to trust me, all because some other officer lied to them. It's not easy trying to rise above dogshit when a person immediately ranks you below it.

Suspects have also told me of officers being very rude or mean to them. My motto is to kill them with kindness. I don't care what kind of crime the person has committed; in my interactions with them, I'm going to treat them with kindness and respect, the way I would want to be treated. As an officer working for the people, it's imperative that I put my personal feelings aside. I can't afford to be judgmental.

By law, everyone is innocent until proven guilty. And that's how I treated Byron from the very beginning: kindly, with understanding and respect. In my opinion, these are the three key building blocks to deal with anyone successfully.

Now, that's not to say every person I deal with is respectful. When I'm disrespected, I still treat that suspect with understanding and respect, but my kindness goes out the window. If someone is a dick to me, I might take it for a short period of time to see if, through our conversation, they change their attitude. But I'll only tolerate it for a little while. If the suspect doesn't change their attitude, then look out, because I will be a dick back to them. I'm glad I never had to take that route with Byron. At the scene, we had both treated each other with dignity. That's why I felt it was so important that I be the one to attempt the statement with Byron: I had built a rapport with him.

When attempting to get a statement, one of the hardest parts of the interview is getting beyond the Miranda rights. The phrase *Miranda warning* was born forty-six years ago, from a US Supreme Court ruling in a landmark case about the Fifth Amendment.

The *Miranda* of *Miranda warning* was Ernesto Miranda. He was arrested in March 1963 in Phoenix, Arizona. While in police custody, he confessed to kidnapping and rape charges. His lawyers sought to overturn his conviction after they learned during a cross-examination that Miranda wasn't told he had the right to a lawyer nor was he told he had the right to remain silent.

The US Supreme Court overturned Miranda's conviction on June 13, 1966, in its ruling for Miranda v. Arizona, which established guidelines for how to inform detained suspects of their constitutional rights.

As a result of Miranda, anyone in police custody must be told four things before being questioned:

1. You have the right to remain silent.
2. Anything you say can and will be used against you in a court of law.
3. You have the right to an attorney.
4. If you cannot afford an attorney, one will be appointed for you.

After reading a suspect their Miranda rights, there's every likelihood the person won't speak to you. This concern was running through my mind with Byron, especially given that Byron had already asked Bill Anderson to help find him an attorney.

I had a strong gut feeling though, that because of the way I had treated Byron during our initial encounter, he may trust me enough to move beyond the Miranda warning. I could sense that Byron wanted to tell his side of the story, but he didn't want to tell just anyone. He wanted to tell the story to me.

At that point, despite being in police custody, Byron had not made any request to speak with an attorney. In fact, he hadn't mentioned the word *attorney* to me.

The fifteen minutes that I sat in my office thinking about all this felt like an hour. I felt like I couldn't wait anymore. I needed to know whether I would be the one interviewing Byron or not.

A minute later, I heard Michel's office door open. He was heading my way. I had butterflies in my stomach, wondering whether I was going to be given the chance to interview my first murder suspect or not.

"I thought it over and decided to let you do the interview with Byron," Michel said. The relief I felt was immediately accompanied by fear. It was on me to get one of the key pieces of evidence in this case.

We had one small interview room in our office. Byron was sitting in there, waiting. There is a small recording room directly next door and a two-way mirror so people can watch the interview without the suspect knowing they're being watched. I knew Michel and other officers would be in that room watching the interview, which only spiked my anxiety further. All eyes were going to be on me, and I didn't want to make any foolish mistakes.

There is a video camera in the interview room, and the digital video recording device and TV monitor are in the recording room next door. The interview is downloaded onto a CD. I grabbed a CD from my office and walked into the recording room to set up the digital video recorder. I put the CD into the machine and tried to turn on the TV monitor. To my horror, the monitor would not turn on! Usually, the monitor is left on, but someone had turned it off and now I couldn't get the damn thing to work. Without the monitor, I couldn't set up the digital video recorder, and so, there'd be no visual recording of the interview. I made sure everything was plugged in. I wiggled all the wires. But it was to no avail; nothing I did worked. Of all times for something to go wrong, that felt like the worst possible moment.

I looked through the two-way mirror at Byron, and he seemed to be getting a little restless. I was worried if I waited any longer, he might get so tired of sitting in that room that he'd refuse to talk to me just so he could get out of there. The only option I had was to use my digital audio recorder instead. That meant only the interview's audio would be recorded. There would be no video. Audio recording is sufficient, but video recording is preferred. It's often beneficial to have a visual to go along with what jurors would be hearing. I had no choice in the matter, though; an audio recording would have to do. I grabbed my audio recorder and a notepad and headed to the interview room.

THE INTERVIEW

I walked into the interview room and closed the door behind me. It was just Byron and me in the room. I set my notepad and digital recorder on the table and asked Byron if he wanted anything to drink, "a cup of coffee, bottle of water, or a pop." Byron declined. I asked him if he needed to use the bathroom and again, he said no.

I asked these questions because I didn't want any distractions once the interview started. I also wanted Byron to know that just because I had arrested him, that didn't mean I didn't care about his well-being. Like I said before, I treat everyone the way I would want to be treated.

I sat down in the chair across from Byron and told him that this would be a recorded conversation. I then turned on the digital recorder. The time was 2:59 p.m.

First, I confirmed Byron's full name and date of birth. Byron was born in June 1948, which made him sixty-four years old. I then confirmed his address, 14319 Elm Street, Little Falls, Minnesota.

When I was a kid, I had watched the *Nightmare on Elm Street* movies. Freddy Krueger was the villain, and those movies gave me nightmares like no other horror movies could. Hearing Byron say he lived on Elm Street caused a chill to run up my spine. After seeing those mutilated teens lying in the basement of Byron's house, I felt like I was sitting across from Freddy Krueger.

Luberts: The reason that led up to why you were placed under arrest was explained to you at the scene, is that correct?

Smith: Because there were bodies and that's a good reason.

Luberts: Now Byron, before I ask you any questions in regard to what had happened, I'm going to read you what's called the Warning and Consent form. These are your Miranda warning legal rights. Have you ever heard of your Miranda warning rights?

Smith: Yeah. Anybody who watches TV hears them.

Luberts: Okay. Byron, before we ask you any questions you must understand what your rights are. You have the right to remain silent. Anything you say can be used against you in court. You have the right to talk to a lawyer for advice before we question you and to have him with you during questioning.

Smith: I understand that, and I waive that considering the circumstances.

Luberts: If you cannot afford a lawyer and want one, a lawyer will be provided for you. If you decide to answer questions now without a lawyer present, you will still have the right to stop answering at any time until you talk to a lawyer. Do you understand that, Byron?

Smith: I understand. I may choose to skip one question or whatever.

Luberts: That's your choice. Yes, by all means, Byron. With your rights in mind, are you willing to talk to me at this time?

Smith: Yes.

Yes! After reading Byron his legal rights, the one simple word I'd been praying to hear came out of Byron's mouth. *Yes.* My gut feeling that Byron would be willing to talk to me was right on the money. Suddenly, an overwhelming feeling of confidence swept over me!

Luberts: Byron, I got called out to your residence today, basically on some information that something might have happened at your house, either today or yesterday.

Smith: More specifically, I called my good friend Bill Anderson who is a neighbor and asked him to contact a lawyer. He wasn't able to; apparently, they were all busy today. The offices were closed. Since he was not able to contact a lawyer, I asked him to contact the Morrison County Sheriff's Department next.

Luberts: How long have you lived at your residence?

Smith: It's been my physical residence since March 2009. However, it has been my home of record since the house was built in September of 1966. It has always been my home.

Luberts: Do you live at the residence with anybody, or do you live by yourself?

Smith: I am by myself.

Luberts: When did you call and talk with Bill Anderson?

Smith: I first called him about 11:30 this morning. Bill is the only person that I have shared the breaking-and-entering series with. As a neighbor I feel it's important and I trust him absolutely. I told him that I had a problem, and I would appreciate it if he got a lawyer and asked him to come over to my house. I don't know the local lawyers very well. Bill seems to know everybody.

Luberts: Was he able to get ahold of a lawyer for you?

Smith: No, he wasn't. He totally failed. He even tried Brainerd.

Luberts: Sure. And just to confirm with you, it's your choice at this time that you wish to waive having an attorney present with you while you talk to me, correct?

Smith: Yes, and if I find anything that I object to, I'll let you know. Immediately and clearly.

Luberts: Okay. Very good. How many times did you talk with Bill Anderson about this today?

Smith: We had back-and-forth phone calls, there must have been ten or twelve when he was calling me with the latest, "Well okay, that didn't work, what next?"

Luberts: Okay. You initially told Bill that somebody broke into your house, is that correct?

Smith: Oh, Bill knew that somebody broke into my house. Yes. He knew that there was a sequence going. He didn't know that it happened again. I tried to be very nonspecific. But he could guess.

Luberts: Did you specifically tell Bill that you had maybe shot somebody that broke into your house or anything?

Smith: No. Bill knows that I was having major problems and that I might do something.

Luberts: So, you've actually been having problems with people breaking into your house, is that correct?

Smith: The same people. The same pattern. It goes back a long time.

Luberts: When did that start, when people were breaking into your house?

Smith: The first time it happened was, I'm guessing, twelve to fifteen years ago and there was a sheriff's report on when they broke into the garage, tore up a bunch of packing cases, threw glass around the floor to break it, and stole a bunch of clothing. Now I try not to be sexist, but when somebody steals clothing and ignores the tools, I tend to think it's a woman.

Luberts: What kind of clothing did they take? Was it women's clothes, men's clothes, or something different?

Smith: Military clothes. You know, the kind of unisex stuff. And not only that but the following week, Ashley Williams was seen wearing my flight line military jacket from the Air Force to school.

Luberts: How do you know Ashley Williams?

Smith: I've never met her.

Luberts: Okay. But you heard that somebody saw her, or you saw her?

Smith: Bill has close relationships with the schools because he does fundraising and he asked, and this was reported to him. However, since it was gossip and rumor it wasn't official evidence. You should check this with him because I want to be totally accurate on it, but I assume he saw her wearing it to the bus.

Luberts: And this was like a camouflage jacket?

Smith: I was in '68 through '72 and at that time everything was olive drab. So, this coat twenty years later was very rare. You know, it's not the sort of thing you would find lying around, and mine was gone and she was seen wearing it, so there was some reasonable suspicion there. And apparently, she was not in full possession of her facilities because she dropped stuff all the way home that Bill collected next morning.

Luberts: From your house?

Smith: Yeah, well stuff had collected in her arms, and it was falling out of her arms on the way home.

Luberts: So, kind of a trail from where she had broken into?

Smith: A trail of dropped stolen stuff she was taking home.

Luberts: Did that trail of dropped stuff, was that in your yard at all?

Smith: Yeah, it was down the driveway. Leading towards their house.

Luberts: So, was Ashley Williams a neighbor of yours?

Smith: My closest neighbor.

Luberts: Do you know Ashley's parents at all?

Smith: I have tried very hard to avoid them. They are nasty people.

Luberts: Okay. You've never gotten along with them?

Smith: I have avoided not getting along with them. They have misused and abused too many other people I know for me to have anything to do with them. I limit myself to being polite.

Luberts: And Ashley, do you know, was she still currently living at home with her parents?

Smith: She's in and out a lot.

Luberts: Was she ever there with a boyfriend that you saw, or any other boy?

Smith: They are too far away from my house to see.

Luberts: So, you've heard and suspect that Ashley Williams had been breaking into your place on different occasions, is that correct to say?

Smith: Yes.

Luberts: Okay. And now in particular you had an incident that happened just recently at your house. A break-in, correct?

Smith: Yeah.

Luberts: When did this happen?

Smith: That would be about three weeks ago. The break-in occurred by kicking in the panel on the basement door. The paneling around the door was shattered, and then they reached through that panel to open up the dead bolt and the knob lock.

Luberts: Were you home at the time this happened?

Smith: No.

Luberts: Do you know if this happened during the day or at night?

Smith: Very specifically, I left to go shopping at St. Cloud 11:30 in the morning, and when I got back at 6:00 the place had been thoroughly gone through. So, I know for sure it happened exactly when I was gone, and it's right down to within the five or six hours, which makes me suspect that it was someone who saw me come and go.

Luberts: Okay.

Smith: Beyond that, the following day, on Sunday, I was at the adjacent property to the north, which I bought as an investment. I had not been there since Thursday. Sometime between Thursday and Sunday afternoon—the break-in at my house was exactly Saturday afternoon. Sometime between Thursday and Sunday afternoon, the garage sidewalk door was kicked open brutally, the frame shattered, lock ruined. Inside the garage, boxes were opened and tipped and dumped. I wasn't keeping anything of value there.

Luberts: Okay.

Smith: So, there was nothing to steal, but the place was made a mess. There's a basement door on the southwest corner of that house. The basement door was kicked in again, frame shattered, locked ruined, and throughout the house, storage closets were left with the doors open and drawers were left half open.

Luberts: Okay. Did you call and report that incident, Byron?

Smith: I turned in a written report to Jamie asking him to investigate. I don't have confirmation that he investigated but I assume he did. I reported the time limits that I observed and the damage that I observed and asked him to verify and document it.

Luberts: Okay.

Smith: There was also a tool bag stolen, actually tools, but it looks like she wanted the bag because there were tools left alongside the bag that weren't taken, but it was a nice bag.

Luberts: So, you suspect a female party stole it?

Smith: It's the same pattern all the way through. And that's years later, after the previous one.

Luberts: Sure.

Smith: So, the house was thoroughly gone through, there's nothing there. It's an empty house that I'm restoring after being vandalized this past spring, but that's a different story, unrelated.

Luberts: Now you told me at your residence today that your house had just been broken into. Can you tell me about that?

Smith: Okay. I had not gone to anyone for Thanksgiving. I am somewhat uncomfortable with other people's family holidays. Some people enjoy it, and it helps them feel homelike. I feel like a little out of place. It's not the kind of social thing I do. So, I was staying at home just because there wasn't anything big happening. I was in the basement in my favorite reading chair reading a paperback.

Luberts: Was this on Thanksgiving Day; is that what you're saying?

Smith: Yeah. This would have been about 12:00, the exact time on the video tape, I mean on the DVR.

Luberts: So, I'm sorry, 12:00 noon?

Smith: Yes.

Luberts: On Thanksgiving Day, which was yesterday, correct? On Thursday?

Smith: Uh-huh.

Luberts: Okay.

Smith: So, that was a very quiet house. It's got electric heat and it's a very quiet house and I hear someone rattling the upstairs door by the garage where everybody comes and goes.

Luberts: Uh-huh.

Smith: This is wrong. You know you shouldn't be rattling doorknobs without at least ringing the doorbell first. So, I set down the book and I'm paying attention and the chair is between the bookshelves, and I see a shadow go past the picture window and then somebody's rattling the basement door trying to get in, but it also is locked and dead bolted. And then I see the shadow in front of the picture window for maybe a half a minute or a minute, like they're trying to see what they can see inside. Okay, this is getting unhappy, and then the shadow leaves and I hear somebody walking across the deck. It's got the wooden planks so you can hear people walk on it and then somebody was rattling the upstairs door and I'm getting seriously stressed because somebody wants in and they're trying to sneak in, and it's happened before. So, I'm sitting there hoping they go away. There's about a minute of silence and I hear a glass window broken, which I later found to be the northwest corner bedroom window.

Luberts: Okay. Where were you at the time in the house when you heard that?

Smith: I was sitting in the same chair in the basement. I consider it my reading chair.

Luberts: That chair, is that the one right off from the bottom of the steps?

Smith: Yeah.

Luberts: Okay.

Smith: Anyway, so I'm in the chair. Now, for the past month my life has been very unhappy. I haven't slept very well. In fact, I'm lucky to get one good night of sleep a month, and I'm keeping everything locked up all the time because I'm being victimized again, and again, and again. And in the past couple weeks I've gotten into the habit of carrying my guns with me inside my house because I don't know who's going to break in when. Oh, it just happened! So, I'm sitting there, and I hear the steps come down the hallway, turn around, and come down the stairs. There are people who've stolen my guns. I figured they're willing to use guns if they steal guns, and I decide that I've got a choice of either shooting or being shot at, which is sort of what I came to when I started carrying them with me. I've been—this past month, I've felt very threatened inside my home.

Luberts: Okay.

41

Smith: And the guy came down the stairs, and I shot him.

Luberts: You said you heard the window break upstairs, correct?

Smith: Uh-huh.

Luberts: You were downstairs. You heard footsteps down the hallway, right?

Smith: Yeah.

Luberts: So, do you think somebody entered in your house through that broken window?

Smith: Oh, absolutely.

Luberts: Okay. So that's how they made entry inside?

Smith: Because it was easier than the dead bolted doors. And I replaced the panel that had been easy to kick out. So, he just decided to break a window instead.

Luberts: How many footsteps did you hear? Did it sound like one person, two people?

Smith: It was definitely one person. Only one person.

Luberts: Okay.

Smith: And after I shot him, I sat down in the chair, and I was tingling with adrenaline. I hate adrenaline. And my blood was pounding in my ears, and I just wanted to calm down more than anything else. And maybe—it's hard to judge the time, two minutes, maybe five minutes I was just sitting there with the blood pounding in my ears, and I hear more footsteps coming down the hallway and somebody else starts down the stairs.

Luberts: Uh-huh.

Smith: And thinking back on it, what happened was, everybody has red buttons. Everybody has sore spots. And I've known since grade school that being ganged up on is a sore spot with me. I just wasn't thinking. I didn't think. I wasn't thinking. I was just; they're ganging up on me, so I killed her too. Same way, except the first shot she tumbled.

Luberts: Okay.

Smith: And I walked over to finish her off. It was a new Mini-14 rifle that I bought to replace the one that had been stolen, and it jammed. My main use for it is muskrats, they destroy the bank, and once in a while, a beaver. They destroy the trees. That's the reason I have it, it's a tool. It had jammed out on the shoreline, which is why I had the .22 with me. It jammed, the trigger clicked, and she laughed at me. I just pulled out the .22 and shot her and shot her. And I sat down again, and I don't think I did anything else for an hour.

Luberts: What time did this happen yesterday?

Smith: It would have been about 12:00.

Luberts: So 12:00 noon yesterday?

Smith: Yeah. And maybe one o'clock or two o'clock I spread the carpets over the blood.

Luberts: Okay. When you said first the male party came in the house after breaking the window in the northeast corner bedroom, and then you heard the footsteps coming down the hallway.

Smith: Yeah.

Luberts: Then immediately did he turn and come down the stairwell or did he go in any other rooms first?

Smith: He came directly down the stairs.

Luberts: Okay. Then you heard footsteps coming down the stairs, is that correct?

Smith: Yes. And then I saw his feet, and then I saw his legs, and when I saw his hips, I shot.

Luberts: Okay. All right. When you shot, what gun were you using at that time?

Smith: The Mini-14.

Luberts: Okay. And you had that with you in the basement when you were sitting in your chair reading, is that correct?

Smith: It was over by the stereo. When I heard the footsteps, I got up and it was maybe five or eight steps away.

Luberts: Do you leave that gun in the basement, loaded, sitting with you?

Smith: No, except for the past couple weeks. The normal location for it is in the closet upstairs in the northeast corner. That's where my parents kept it. I kept it there too. It's the easiest place to get it if you see a muskrat in the river.

Luberts: Okay.

Smith: Home defense has never been an issue until recently.

Luberts: So, was your Mini-14 sitting in the basement, loaded, at the time this male party came and broke into your house?

Smith: I always keep it loaded.

Luberts: Okay. How many rounds do you keep in the gun?

Smith: Since it jammed, three or four. That's all it'll hold maximum.

Luberts: Okay. And then you said you also had a .22 revolver pistol, what kind of gun was that?

Smith: It's a revolver.

Luberts: How many shots is that?

Smith: It's a nine-shot. It's a wood hand grip, somewhat dark, and a standard blued finish.

Luberts: Okay. And did you have it in a holster or a gun case or anything?

Smith: Brown leather holster. I'd actually been wearing that inside the house somewhat regularly.

Luberts: Were you wearing it at the time the break-in occurred?

Smith: Yeah. The brown leather holster has a belt loop and I had it on my right-side hip.

Luberts: And was it loaded when you had it?

Smith: Yes, it was. In fact, it was still loaded when they found it. They should have found it on the closet shelf upstairs. If not, they should pick it up because I don't want to leave it lying loose with nobody in the house.

Luberts: Okay. You said you had used that .22 to shoot the female party, is that correct?

Smith: Yeah. I might have put one—I'm trying—I don't remember clearly whether the final shot to the man in the face was with that or not.

Luberts: Okay.

Smith: I don't want to prolong the suffering even if I kill somebody. I don't want to leave them lay and suffer. In fact, with the female, after I dragged her out of the way she was still doing some faint gasping and I just right there.

Luberts: You're saying "right there" but you're pointing your finger underneath your chin?

Smith: Up in the chin into the cranium. The .22 is a pea shooter; it doesn't go through bone very well.

Luberts: Okay. Just to clarify with you, first we'll clarify with the male party. He was walking down the steps, after you heard him coming down the hallway.

Smith: Yeah.

Luberts: He was walking down the steps to go to the basement. You saw his feet first, then his knees, and then his hips, correct?

Smith: Yeah. And I shot him somewhere in the hip area.

Luberts: Okay. How many times did you shoot when you saw his hip coming down the steps?

Smith: It might have been twice. I think it was once, but it might have been twice.

Luberts: Okay. Did this male party have anything in his hands at all when he was walking down the steps when you saw him? Or did you even see his hands at that point?

Smith: I didn't see his hands at that point.

Luberts: Okay. So, he's coming down the steps, you shoot twice. Can you tell me what he was wearing, what kind of clothes he was wearing?

Smith: He was dressed like a high schooler but much too old. Ah, fancy belt, and jeans.

Luberts: What did he have for a shirt or maybe a jacket, did you see? Do you recall?

Smith: That's blank. I'm blank on that.

Luberts: Okay.

Smith: One thing of importance: his shoes came off.

Luberts: Okay.

Smith: His shoes I kicked underneath the reading chair, and they're still there.

Luberts: Okay. Do you know what kind of shoes they are?

Smith: I checked the tread pattern on purpose. Whoever kicked in the door the previous time left their tread pattern on the door and I brought it in to Jamie the following day. He saved it in the evidence file. It had a sawtooth repeated pattern on the door and that is characteristic of skateboard shoes. I pointed it out to Jamie, pointing out as a piece of evidence that very few people over thirty wear skateboard shoes.

Luberts: Uh-huh.

Smith: I like them because they're the best shoe for city hiking so I showed him a pair, showed him the tread pattern, and I said, "Watch for this."

Luberts: Okay.

Smith: The shoes that I kicked under the chair had that tread pattern.

Luberts: So those were the same shoes that the male party was wearing when he came into your house?

Smith: He was wearing them yesterday. They dropped off. I checked the tread pattern, and it looked to me to match the pattern on the door panel.

Luberts: Okay.

Smith: People lose their balance on the stairs when they're shot.

Luberts: Sure.

Smith: And he tumbled down to the floor.

Luberts: Is that when the shoes fell off of him?

Smith: Yes.

Luberts: Okay. So now you shoot twice with the Mini-14, you hit him in the hip area, is that where you hit him?

Smith: Yeah.

Luberts: He falls down to the bottom of the steps and he's on the floor, correct?

Smith: And he's looking face up at me.

Luberts: Okay. Then what?

Smith: I shoot him in the face.

Luberts: Okay.

Smith: I want him dead.

Luberts: Uh-huh. Where in the face did you shoot him, do you remember?

Smith: I don't know exactly. Somewhere near the center and I didn't check afterwards.

Luberts: Okay. And was that with the Mini-14 that you shot him in the face?

Smith: I think so.

Luberts: Okay.

Smith: Now, at that point there was a lot of blood, and I had a tarp lying by the fireplace that I was going to use to cover up the firewood. I pulled him on the tarp to keep so much blood from soaking into the carpet.

Luberts: Okay. So, did you pull him over by, out, away from the bottom of the steps over towards the fireplace?

Smith: Ah, no, I spread the tarp out and pulled him onto the tarp. I might have moved him two or three feet.

Luberts: Where did you move him from there, from the bottom of the steps?

Smith: Ah, it would have been slightly towards the fireplace because that's where I laid out the tarp.

Luberts: Okay.

Smith: Then I just wanted it out of my sight, and I dragged him around the corner into the shop.

Luberts: In the shop area that's set up in the basement, correct?

Smith: Which is exactly where you found him.

Luberts: Okay. Then when did the female party come in? Was this after this had happened?

Smith: Before, I said two to five minutes later, and since I was just sitting there stunned that's the best estimate I can give. Two to five minutes.

Luberts: Then you said you were sitting there, stunned, after this had happened. Where were you sitting?

Smith: Same chair.

Luberts: In the same chair. Okay. And then tell me what happened?

Smith: And the rifle was sitting right alongside me at that time because I had just used it.

Luberts: And you fired three rounds; did you reload the gun?

Smith: Possibly four. I am not sure how many were in it and then I reloaded it, yes.

Luberts: Okay. Did you have a box of ammunition sitting there, or did you have rounds in your pants pocket, or did you have to go get the rounds to reload it?

Smith: They were on the countertop above the stereo. I just had some loose rounds there.

Luberts: Okay. How many rounds do you recall putting back in to reload the Mini-14? How many rounds did you put back in, do you remember?

Smith: The magazine only holds three and there was one in the chamber. So, I would have put in three.

Luberts: Uh-huh.

Smith: And that's why it misfired after the first shot.

Luberts: Oh, okay.

Smith: So, the first shot as she was coming down the stairs, as I recall, was again at about hip height and she fell, and it repeated except—

Luberts: Hold on, if that's okay. How many times did you shoot when you saw the hip area coming down the stairs, her hip area?

Smith: I'm quite sure it would have been only once, because it's the second shot that jams coming out of the magazine.

Luberts: Okay. And did you hit her with that first shot, do you remember?

Smith: I don't know. I was shaking pretty hard. I might have missed. I mean, it's what I would consider point-blank range, but I can't say for sure I hit her.

Luberts: Okay.

Smith: She did tumble, though.

Luberts: Was that after the first shot that she tumbled?

Smith: Yes.

Luberts: So, odds are you probably did hit her then?

Smith: Yeah. Or I might have just grazed her.

Luberts: Okay. And, again, you saw the feet first coming down the steps, correct?

Smith: Yes.

Luberts: From the chair, and then when it reached where you could see her hip area, that's when you fired first? And obviously you didn't see her hands at that time?

Smith: My thinking—no.

Luberts: Or if she had anything in her hands?

Smith: My thinking was, I'm not going to ask if there's a gun.

Luberts: Right.

Smith: You know, people who steal guns, I don't want to give them the chance to shoot me.

Luberts: Yeah.

Smith: She could have or might not have had a gun in her hands.

Luberts: Okay.

Smith: And if there's one in the corner somewhere, or if it was inside her clothing, or her purse, I didn't check.

Luberts: Okay. So, you shot, she came tumbling down the steps, and then you went to shoot again, and the gun jammed, is that correct?

Smith: Yes.

Luberts: Okay. Now what happened after that, after the gun jammed?

Smith: After the gun jammed—well, he fell with his head under the table; she fell immediately at the bottom of the steps, so you'll see two different patches of blood on the floor.

Luberts: Okay.

Smith: And when the gun clicked, misfired, she laughed at me.

Luberts: When she was laughing at you, she was at the bottom of the steps on the floor?

Smith: It wasn't a very long laugh because she was already hurting, but you know, there was this, okay—there was another red button I guess most people would have, so if you're trying to shoot somebody and they laugh at you, you go again.

Luberts: So, when she laughed at you, did that—how did that make you feel? Did that infuriate you, or make you upset, or?

Smith: I knew that the gun had misfired previously. I take care of it. I was ready, and I just pulled it out, and yes, I fired more shots than I needed to.

Luberts: Okay. Why did you fire more shots than you needed to?

Smith: The .22 is a pea shooter, and I was very, very threatened, unhappy.

Luberts: You were mad, correct?

Smith: Yes.

Luberts: Okay. She had basically enraged you for laughing at you. Do you think that was part of it?

Smith: No, that was just, that was incidental. She'd been a—whoever it was who was breaking into my home had been doing it for so long that I was no longer willing to live in fear.

Luberts: Okay. So, it was kind of, correct me if I'm wrong, Byron, but it seems like a combination of things that made you mad basically at that point, would that be fair to say?

Smith: Oh, I was far over the edge.

Luberts: Okay. When you say far over the edge, how do you mean? Are you referring to infuriated?

Smith: No.

Luberts: Upset or how were you feeling?

Smith: Normally, when I do something, I justify it. Normally, when I do something, I know exactly why I'm doing it and what I expect. I was reacting.

Luberts: Okay. What were you reacting to is what I'm asking?

Smith: The threat. The previous losses.

Luberts: Okay.

Smith: I spent twenty years overseas. A couple years in Bangkok, several years in Cairo, several years in nasty sub-Saharah Africa, three years in Moscow, and three years in Beijing.

Luberts: Did you ever have to kill anyone before, Byron?

Smith: No. I was never threatened. I never had anything stolen. There was never any vandalism. Twenty years overseas, not one problem.

Luberts: Uh-huh.

Smith: And I retire to my peaceful hometown.

Luberts: Okay. Not to dwell on it, Byron, but I almost got the story. With the female party, she had fallen to the ground, she laughed, she kind of had this laugh, like you said, when your gun misfired, and then you said you reached towards your hip; you had the .22 on you, correct?

Smith: I was wearing the .22. I have been wearing it inside my house for the past several weeks.

Luberts: Right. And that was loaded and it's a nine-shot you said, correct?

Smith: Yes.

Luberts: Okay. You pulled the .22 and what'd you do with it?

Smith: It was partially empty. So, the first round, there wasn't a bullet in for the first time I pulled the trigger, and I normally keep it that way. That's a minor safety thing. I can always pull the trigger again.

Luberts: Where were you aiming, do you recall?

Smith: Probably at her heart.

Luberts: Okay.

Smith: And then she stopped moving.

Luberts: Did the gun go off when you were aiming at her heart?

Smith: Oh yes. Yes, maybe the chest area, I wasn't aiming that accurately.

Luberts: Okay.

Smith: I would guess there were about four shots with the .22.

Luberts: Okay.

Smith: And she stopped moving, so I grabbed her by the clothing and dragged her over onto the tarp that was in the shop. That's where I left her.

Luberts: When you shot her, you said four times, one was in the chest. Where were the other three rounds, do you know?

Smith: I would assume they were nearby.

Luberts: Near the chest—in the chest area or?

Smith: In the upper chest.

Luberts: Okay. Did you shoot her in the facial area or head area at all?

Smith: After she was on the tarp she was still gasping. And as much as I hate someone, I don't believe they deserve pain, so I gave her a shot under the chin up into the cranium.

Luberts: Was she still at the bottom of the stairwell when that happened?

Smith: No. That was over in the shop.

Luberts: Oh, that was in the shop?

Smith: Yeah. I thought she was dead, and it turned out she wasn't. So, I did a good, clean finishing shot.

Luberts: Okay.

Smith: And she gave out the death twitch. First time I've ever seen it in a human, but it works the same in beaver, and deer, and whatever.

Luberts: Uh-huh. Okay. Like I said, I asked you before if she had anything in her hands when she was walking down the steps, but you said you never saw anything in her hands, correct?

Smith: I never saw her hands. She tumbled before I saw her hands. Her hands were open, but she would have dropped anything she was carrying and if there was something tangled up in her clothing or not, I didn't check.

Luberts: Okay. Did she drop anything though? You moved her body, so did you notice if she dropped anything?

Smith: There was nothing she dropped that I saw on the floor after I moved her.

Luberts: Okay.

Smith: If it had gotten her—her clothing was very tangled. In fact, her clothing was sufficiently tangled that in the shop her breasts were exposed, and I pulled her shirt down again.

Luberts: Okay. So, Byron, she fell to the ground, you shot once with the M-14?

Smith: Yeah.

Luberts: She came tumbling down the steps. Now she's at the bottom of the steps. She basically didn't have anything in her hands.

Smith: I wasn't looking at her hands.

Luberts: Okay.

Smith: I wasn't looking at any of the details.

Luberts: But she's laying there, correct?

Smith: Yes.

Luberts: Obviously you had hit her, so she's hurt, correct?

Smith: Yes. Well, I didn't know how well I hit her. I mean, she was still laying there looking at me; she could have gotten up again for all I know.

Luberts: Okay. My question, Byron, is why did you shoot again? She didn't have a weapon in her hand.

Smith: Actually, I didn't know if she had a weapon in her hand until later.

Luberts: But she was laying there hurt, she wasn't threatening you, I'm just, I have to ask you.

Smith: I thought she was threatening me.

Luberts: Okay. Explain that to me.

Smith: I assumed she had a gun. Either inside something, or in the purse, or in her hand, or whatever, and I'm not going to wait for her to—I'm not going to ask her if she has a gun.

Luberts: Right. Understandable. Okay.

Smith: I'm not going to wait until she shows it or if she uses it while I'm looking for it. I had already determined that both of them were gun thieves. As far as I was concerned, they were totally dangerous.

Luberts: Okay. All right. And this happened, you said, with both parties at around noon yesterday, correct?

Smith: Yeah. Maybe five- or ten-minute gap between them.

Luberts: What was she wearing?

Smith: That was memorable. A tight black sweatshirt that said "Hard Candy," and when I saw that I said, "Yeah, you're hard." And she is well-known throughout the community as a hard case.

Luberts: Okay.

Smith: Vandalism in Belle Prairie, etc. Anyway, it was something like a sweatshirt, black, but better than that, she had the drawstring tight around her face.

Luberts: Okay. So, she had the hood up?

Smith: Oh yes. And tightly drawn around to disguise any visual characteristics.

Luberts: Okay.

Smith: The reason that struck me is that I had put up cameras to get visual characteristics of whoever it was, and she had already prepared herself to not be identified. Subsequently, thinking about it, I became very upset that all of this surveillance effort could have been for nothing because she was so well covered up, it probably wouldn't have even been good enough to take the case to court.

Luberts: Okay. Do you remember what kind of pants she was wearing, or shoes?

Smith: I remember the shoes because I was still checking for skateboard shoes, and she was wearing some sort of winter boot that was something else.

Luberts: Okay.

Smith: But it was after that since she was wearing some sort of winter boot, black and white, with some sort of pattern, that I checked his shoes and saw the pattern there because hers didn't have the pattern. I assumed since it was a smaller wave pattern that it was somebody with a small foot. But then I noticed on his shoes that the outside was smooth, so it would have only printed in the small wave pattern.

Luberts: Okay.

Smith: So that needs to be carefully looked at to see if he was the one who kicked in the door earlier. And

I've got every reason to believe that they were working as a pair.

Luberts: Okay.

Smith: Well, as she went along the hall, she rattled the doorknob on the front door. Apparently, she expected him to open the door to let her in.

Luberts: Okay.

Smith: That's just a suspicion. I wasn't there watching, but why would you rattle the doorknob if you're already inside the house unless you're wondering why it wasn't unlocked?

Luberts: So, did you hear the doorknob after the window was broken, or before?

Smith: Oh, there were two sets. The first time around was apparently just him, all three doors, window break, walking downstairs. She showed up several minutes later. I don't know what I would have done if they'd come down at the same time.

Luberts: Okay.

Smith: That's a what-if.

Luberts: Okay.

Smith: But anyway, she came in maybe five minutes later and walked down the hall. She rattled the doorknob like she was curious why it hadn't been opened. Like she expected him to let her in. They were obviously accustomed to working with each other.

Luberts: Okay. Now you said you put both of them on the tarp and you drug both?

Smith: No. I dragged him in on the tarp.

Luberts: Yes.

Smith: And then she came down later, and I dragged her onto the tarp afterwards.

Luberts: Okay. Yeah.

Smith: That was mostly just to minimize the amount of blood in the carpet. I'm going to replace the carpet anyway.

Luberts: Okay. And then you drug her back in right by him, is that correct, the male party?

Smith: Yes. And shut the door so I didn't have to see them.

Luberts: Okay. And that's where they both were at when we came to your house and you pointed out to us, showed us that's where they were, correct?

Smith: Yeah.

Luberts: Okay.

Smith: The only thing that I did about an hour later was put my fingers to the vein to see if it was pulsing. It wasn't.

Luberts: On who?

Smith: Both of them. I just, you know, sitting there in the chair, okay, I don't want to do it, but I got to check.

Luberts: Okay. And you were checking to see if what? To make—

Smith: If I had—if they were still alive.

Luberts: Okay.

Smith: You know the things that run through your mind when you're sitting there afterwards.

Luberts: Uh-huh. So, after you, both bodies are in that back-office room, what did you go do?

Smith: The rest of the evening, the rest of that afternoon, that evening, all night long, and the next morning, I was afraid of an accomplice. Bill and I had already discussed this, that they probably had somebody in their house watching to see if I come driving home, to see if they see me, to see if anybody else is coming in. You know, "Hey, get out [of] there. There's somebody coming in." So, Bill and I really thought that their parents were in on it.

Luberts: Oh, okay.

Smith: This was pure speculation, but to us it seemed reasonable, and I was sitting there afraid that most likely the brass-plated bitch would nag Scott into it, and he would come over with a gun to see what had gone wrong. I was sitting there afraid.

Luberts: Okay.

Smith: And by this noon, I had finally reached the point where nothing's happened. I'm not going to be afraid anymore, let's get this over with.

Luberts: Okay. So that's when you called Bill, right?

Smith: Yep.

Luberts: Right after everything happened, it's done—

Smith: I sat there for maybe two hours. The blood was pounding in my ears.

Luberts: And where did you sit?

Smith: Back in the reading chair.

Luberts: Okay. And then after two hours, then what did you do? Were you home the entire time after this happened?

Smith: I was in the basement, hiding in the basement the entire time.

Luberts: Okay. Did you leave the residence at all from when the incident happened up until my arrival at your home?

Smith: Never. No.

Luberts: Okay.

Smith: That was the first time I unlocked the door.

Luberts: So, you were home the entire time?

Smith: Yes. In fact, I was afraid to go upstairs because I thought there might be somebody with a gun looking in the windows.

Luberts: Okay.

Smith: I was hiding in that chair. You may have found my other hiding place in the back of the storeroom. When I fell over backwards and knocked my head and got that scab, I landed on my tailbone and it hurt to sit in that same chair for more than an hour or two, so I alternated between that chair and a chair in the back of the storeroom.

Luberts: Okay. And then when we came and made contact with you at your house, you went through the scene with us and showed us what you had.

Smith: Yep.

Luberts: Showed us where the bodies were, and I told

you that I had placed you under arrest at that time and took you into custody, correct?

Smith: Yes.

Luberts: Okay. And then I did a quick pat down search of you, is that correct?

Smith: Yes.

Luberts: For officer safety reasons. And then you had approximately four shells, I believe they were the Mini-14 rounds in your pocket, is that correct?

Smith: I took the rest of them off the counter that the stereo was on and put them in my pocket in case the gun jammed in the back room or whatever, cause I was carrying it with me every step.

Luberts: Okay.

Smith: The entire time.

Luberts: So, you had approximately four rounds of the Mini-14 in your right pocket when I did a pat down search of you. Would that be fair to say?

Smith: Yes. There were about four in my pocket. It might have been five.

Luberts: Okay. And then in your left front pocket I actually found approximately about the same, four to five rounds of .22 shells. Would that be fair to say?

Smith: Yes.

Luberts: Okay. And I placed those actually on the table in the basement next to where we had met.

Smith: Yes. I felt very at threat because in my opinion, Scott Williams is semi-psychotic, and he attacked numerous people for obscure reasons, and I, if he was the person watching, if he was being an accomplice, he would come down with a gun to solve whatever problem he received. I felt totally at threat. In fact, I'm going to sleep safer tonight here.

Luberts: Uh-huh. Byron, what clothes were you wearing when this happened, when you had shot these two that entered into your—broke into your home?

Smith: After it got dark in the late evening, I snuck upstairs to my bedroom, got these pants and took off the brown pants, same model Wranglers, and rolled them up and stuffed them in the back corner behind the shelf that holds the stereo equipment. They're still there.

Luberts: In your bedroom, you're saying?

Smith: No.

Luberts: Oh.

Smith: In the basement. I just stuffed them out of the way.

Luberts: Okay. So, they're in the basement and you stuffed them, you said, where? I'm sorry.

Smith: The reading chair, the stairway, the stereo equipment, around on the east side of the stereo equipment on the north side of the room against the north wall, which is the center divider wall of the house.

Luberts: Okay. Is it kind of behind the stairs?

Smith: It's underneath the stairs, except at the top of the stairs there's a landing, so it's underneath the landing where you enter the stairs.

Luberts: Got ya. Okay. And you said they're like a brown-in-color jeans?

Smith: Right. Same as these Wranglers, my standard brand, standard size. Thinking of it now, don't get confused on the analysis, someone gave me a couple beaver that he trapped in my yard. They're terrible on the trees, and one leg has a bunch of beaver blood on it.

Luberts: Okay.

Smith: So, there's both beaver blood and human blood on the pants.

Luberts: Oh, okay. Okay.

Smith: Just in case anybody analyzes it.

Luberts: Right. Yeah. What were you wearing for shoes, then?

Smith: Exactly the same as I have now.

Luberts: Okay. So, you were wearing shoes at the time that this happened, correct?

Smith: I was. I've been wearing all of this exactly as I have now, except I changed the pants sometime around midnight.

Luberts: Okay. So, you had the blue-jean coat on also? When this happened?

Smith: Yeah. I keep the house cool. I always wear an overcoat, or I mean a heavy shirt in the wintertime.

Luberts: Okay. So, you didn't change your shirt or your jacket at all then since it happened?

Smith: There might be spots on here.

Luberts: Yeah, that's why I'm asking.

Smith: Yeah.

Luberts: So, you're saying there might be spots of blood on your jean jacket that you're wearing, correct?

Smith: Yes.

Luberts: Okay. How about the blue shirt you have on?

Smith: Same shirt, the tails were out at that time. I tucked them in now.

Luberts: Okay.

Smith: I tucked them in when I changed pants. So, there might be spots of blood on the tails of the shirt. I don't see any here and the sleeves of the jacket would have covered the shirt.

Luberts: Okay. I'm going to need your clothes for analysis. Do you have any problems if I take possession of your clothes for any evidence reasons?

Smith: Check them for anything you want.

Luberts: So, you have no problem if I would obtain them right now at this point?

Smith: No. I would like to have something else to wear.

Luberts: Yes, you will.

Smith: Okay.

Luberts: But you don't object to me holding on to your clothes for evidence at this point?

Smith: No. I have plenty of spare clothes.

Luberts: Okay.

Smith: In fact, I noticed that there is a spot of blood on the tip of the shoes.

Luberts: Yeah. I had kind of noticed. I see that right here now when you're talking to me about it.

Smith: Yeah.

Luberts: Okay. So, I will have to obtain those for evidence reasons, and you're okay with that?

Smith: I understand that there are procedures to be followed and these procedures are all established for well-justified reasons, and I don't intend to argue with any of it.

Luberts: Okay. Sounds good, Byron. Byron, I would also like to ask you, would you be okay to consent to give me a DNA test?

Smith: No problem at all.

Luberts: And the way I would obtain that is by a mouth, cheek swab.

Smith: I'm familiar with the process. Yeah.

Luberts: Would you consent to giving me one of those?

Smith: Yes.

Luberts: Yes. Okay.

Smith: Also, you should get a new print of that. It's healed up since Jamie took mine a couple weeks ago.

Luberts: Are you saying your thumb print?

Smith: Yeah. You've got a full set except for the thumb, but we'll do it again.

Luberts: Okay. You'd be willing to do that for us?

Smith: Sure.

Luberts: Okay.

Smith: I mean, I've done it already.

Luberts: Sure. So, if it's okay with you, I would like to obtain, when I'm done talking to you, a DNA sample from you, a cheek swabbing, mouth swabbing. That's the DNA sample, and then I'd like to obtain a full set of fingerprints from you. Are you willing to consent to me to do that?

Smith: I consent to all of that.

Luberts: Okay. Thank you very much.

Smith: And actually, they might come out better because I haven't been doing as much yard work the past couple weeks.

Luberts: Sure. Now Byron, when I got to your house, you told us, also after I had placed you into custody, that the guns were in your upstairs closet, correct?

Smith: In the northeast corner of the house, but actually there are two closets and there was the—well, you can tell where the rifle goes because the wall right there is scarred from twenty years of it.

Luberts: Okay. Yeah.

Smith: And the handgun was in the right-hand closet.

Luberts: Okay. So, you had the .22 handgun in the right-hand closet, correct?

Smith: Uh-huh, on the top shelf.

Luberts: And then you had the Mini-14 in the left-hand closet.

Smith: Leaning up against the left side of the left-hand closet.

Luberts: Okay. When did you put those guns in the closet?

Smith: When you were on your way.

Luberts: Okay.

Smith: I don't like to have guns in sight anytime law enforcement is involved because it makes you guys nervous.

Luberts: Oh yeah. Very true. Yeah.

Smith: And that's why I came to the door with my hands out and up.

Luberts: Yeah. Yes, you did, and I appreciate that. How did you know that we were on the way to your house?

Smith: Oh, Bill called me; he said you'd be there in five or ten minutes.

Luberts: Okay.

Smith: But I know Bill enough to know that five, ten minutes and it actually took you twenty-five. So, I wasn't worrying about it. Bill's numbers are a little loose.

Luberts: Okay. Sure.

Smith: But I knew you'd come. Actually, I was sitting at the kitchen table watching down the driveway, which is why I was ready for you at the door.

Luberts: Okay. I have to ask, Byron: after the shooting and it's done, why didn't you call law enforcement to report what happened?

Smith: For the first couple hours I was just shaking, and I gradually shifted into worrying about another accomplish, I mean accomplice. There'd already been two.

Luberts: Uh-huh.

Smith: Who knew that both the brass-plated bitch and her husband were both watching.

Luberts: Uh-huh.

Smith: As far as I knew, the whole family was in on it. Bill and I thought the whole family were in on it, and I was pretty much afraid to do anything. An hour later I had this screwball thought that it seems sort of irrational now, but just because my Thanksgiving's screwed up, I don't need to screw up yours.

Luberts: Okay. Is that kind of why you didn't call law enforcement?

Smith: That-that-that—that was a part of it, and I was also sitting there thinking it's all over; it's not going to change. I can wait until tomorrow in the daylight. I might be thinking more clearly.

Luberts: Okay.

Smith: I saw it as a static situation.

Luberts: Sure. Okay. Byron, I think we covered pretty much what I can think of at this point.

Smith: And I—okay, and I haven't thought of anything else to add, but if I do, I'll let you know.

Luberts: Okay.

Smith: Details like the shoes might pop up later.

Luberts: Sure.

Smith: Details like making sure the DVR is turned off before tomorrow noon.

Luberts: Okay. If we have any further questions later with you, would you be okay to talk with us later?

Smith: Absolutely.

Luberts: Okay. Then I'm going to conclude this statement at this time.

Smith: Okay.

Luberts: Does that sound good, Byron?

Smith: Uh-huh.

Luberts: Okay. And the time right now is 4:01 p.m.

THE SECOND
INTERVIEW

I told Byron I'd be back in a few minutes, then I stood up and walked out of the interview room. I felt relieved at how well the interview had gone. A great sense of accomplishment swept over me.

Sheriff Wetzel and two BCA agents were standing by the interview room door as I walked out. I talked with the lead BCA agent, Chad Museus, who had watched some of the interview, and Sheriff Wetzel, who had watched the whole interview. They asked me to go back in and ask Byron about the guns he said were stolen from his residence. They wanted me to get clarification about those weapons.

I went to my office and got a DNA kit consisting of two Q-tip cotton swabs in an envelope. Since he'd already consented to it, I planned to obtain a DNA sample from Byron when I got done talking to him.

I then walked back into the interview room and informed Byron I had more questions I would like to ask him regarding the guns he said were stolen and the previous break-ins. I activated my digital recorder at 4:19 p.m. I confirmed with Byron that I had read to him his Miranda rights earlier, and he said I had, and that he understood them.

Byron said, "This is a reasonable continuation of an important matter." I asked Byron, with his rights in mind, if he would be willing to continue to talk with me, and he said yes.

Byron reported he had previous break-ins to his house and items had been stolen. I asked him if guns had been taken from his house on those break-in complaints and he said yes. I asked Byron if the particular guns that were used in the shooting had been at his house during the past burglaries. He told me the first couple were not break-ins, but thefts. He said that during one of the break-ins, they missed the guns, but the second time, they found two guns in the closet. He said he had a stainless-steel Ruger Mini-14 stolen from him. Byron told me after the gun was stolen, he went to Walmart and bought a replacement. He said a shotgun was also stolen. It had been his father's, and he had used it for thirty to forty years of happy hunting.

Byron told me he purchased the Ruger Mini-14 that he used in the incident three weeks ago, a couple of days after the previous break-in, to replace the one that had been stolen. He told me he had owned the .22 revolver since 1975. I asked him, regarding the previous break-ins, if someone didn't see that .22 and missed it.

"That's how I knew some of the other possible neighbors who might have been nosy were made very unlikely. Because in the back corner of that closet there was a gun that was in the case, and this thief was sufficiently unfamiliar with guns to just take the ones that were identified as you could see they were guns. She missed the one that was in a case," Byron said.

Byron told me most guy hunters can tell whether a gun is in a case or not, but this person took the two that weren't in a case and missed the one in the back corner. I asked him if it was the .22 he was referring to that they missed, and he told me, "No, they missed the 30.06 rifle," a gun he had purchased about a year before. After more conversation with Byron, I was finally able to confirm that according to him, the reason the .22 hadn't been taken in the previous break-ins was because the thief had missed it. I then concluded my statement with Byron at 4:25 p.m.

Byron had given me verbal consent to obtain a DNA sample from him during our recorded interview, but I wanted to make doubly sure that any evidence I obtained was obtained legally so that I didn't lose it later in court. Defense attorneys love to try to nitpick at any little thing they can to get evidence thrown out. To avoid this situation, I used a consent-to-search form to ask Byron, once again, to consent to me obtaining his DNA sample via a mouth/cheek swab. Byron read the form and signed it, giving me consent to obtain the sample.

I put on my rubber gloves to make sure I wouldn't cross-contaminate any evidence. I checked Byron's mouth to verify that he didn't have anything in it, and I took the Q-tip swabs to both sides of his cheeks, inside his mouth. A mouth/cheek swab collects skin cells from inside the mouth, and those cells contain that person's DNA. I put the swabs back in their container and sealed it in the envelope provided with the collection kit.

I stood up and told Byron that we were done for the moment, and that it was time to walk him over to the jail. Byron said okay, and then stood up and followed me out of the interview room to the lobby of the sheriff's office. We walked out of the lobby and across the hallway to where the jail entry door is. I secured my gun in the gun locker next to the entry door since no firearms are allowed in the jail. Then I pushed the intercom button. One of the correctional officers responded, and I told him I had one in custody to bring into the jail. The entry doors to the jail are steel. They have locking mechanisms that are controlled by the correctional officers who work in the jail's master control tower. The door opened, and I walked Byron into the jail entryway. From there, it's two flights up to the jail's booking room. While walking up the stairs, Byron said, "I'm going to sleep much better tonight knowing that I will be safe."

When we reached the booking room, the door opened and we went inside. I secured the steel door behind us. The doors lock automatically, and because they are steel, they make a loud metal slamming noise when they close. When that happens, the prisoner we brought into jail knows that they are there to stay. I've had a lot of them tell me it's the worst noise they have ever heard. Byron, on the other hand, looked like he was comforted by the noise.

I walked over to the computer and started booking Byron into the jail. The correctional officer asked me what the charges were. I told him, "Two counts of second-degree murder."

He laughed, then said, "No, really. What are the charges?"

I again said, "Two counts of second-degree murder." He looked at Byron, then looked at me and said, "Really, you're not joking?"

"Really, it's not a joke."

He had a "holy shit" look on his face when he booked Byron into the jail. In our county, it's not common to have to bring someone to jail for murder.

You might be wondering why I didn't book Byron into jail for two counts of first-degree murder. A person cannot be charged with first-degree murder until there's been a grand jury. The grand jury must decide whether there is enough probable cause for someone to be charged with first-degree murder.

Another thing most people don't understand is that law enforcement does the booking charge for people brought into jail, but that doesn't necessarily mean that's the crime they're going to be criminally prosecuted for. The county attorney's office reviews each case and decides what the actual criminal charge will be. It's the county attorney's office that does the criminal charging, not law enforcement. The booking charge made by the arresting officer is tantamount to a suggestion of what criminal charge the suspect could or should face.

The booking process took me about ten minutes, then I left the jail. I walked out feeling accomplished. At least for a little while, Byron was in custody, and so justice had been served for the two teenage victims.

SEARCH WARRANTS AND IDENTITY OF THE TEENAGERS

I walked back into the office and met with Agent Museus and Sheriff Wetzel.

"We still don't know for sure who the two teenagers are that Byron killed. It sounds to me that Byron suspects the female is his neighbor, Ashley Olson. He didn't mention anything about who the boy might be," I told them.

Sheriff Wetzel said dispatch received a phone call from family members of two teenage cousins, Nicholas Brady and Haile Kifer, who hadn't shown up for Thanksgiving dinner at their parents' house. The parents couldn't reach them on their cell phones, and no one had heard from them or seen them since yesterday.

I recognized the name *Nicholas Brady* because I had been recently investigating thefts and burglaries in other parts of the county and his name came up as a person of interest. I had no evidence to prove he was involved in anything, but he was on my radar.

I was not familiar with the name *Haile Kifer*. I hadn't heard or seen her name mentioned in anything I'd worked on. I knew there was a good chance these were the teenagers lying dead in Byron's basement.

I called the Morrison County Attorney, Brian Middendorf, and his assistant, Todd Kosovich, and told them about what we had. They both agreed to come down to the sheriff's office to assist us with the case.

In the meantime, we received a call from local State Patrol Officer Bryan Bearce. Bryan had heard that we'd arrested Byron for killing two teenagers, and he told us he had something rather interesting to share with us. We asked Patrol Sergeant Shawn Larson to follow up with Bryan. Shawn drove to Bryan's residence to meet with him.

Bryan told Shawn about a 1995 gray Chevy S-10 pickup that had been parked in front of his residence on Oak Lane since yesterday. Oak Lane is a dead end cul-de-sac located approximately a quarter mile north of Byron's residence.

On November 22, Thanksgiving Day, at approximately 4:12 p.m., Bryan said he received a phone call from his wife, Karla. Karla was also a local state patrol officer. Karla told Bryan that the pickup had been parked in their yard, on the grass, facing west. The vehicle was registered to Byron Smith. The pickup was still parked there, in the same location as the prior day, when Shawn arrived. Shawn had the pickup towed to our sheriff's office impound garage.

I immediately wondered if Byron had parked his pickup away from his residence to make it look like he wasn't home, if he had set the whole thing up, wanting to catch the people that were breaking into his residence so badly, that he had taken steps to make it look like he wasn't home.

Byron sat downstairs in his home waiting for someone to break in so he could get his revenge. The weird things that he told me in his statement about the shoes under his reading chair matching the shoe tread on the door panel from his previous burglary, the way he shot the boy in the face because he wanted him dead, the way he shot the girl multiple times after he claims she laughed at him, the energy bars and bottles of water sitting by his reading chair, and the fact that he had not called law enforcement to report what happened, all made sense with the discovery of that vehicle. He had it planned all along; he was going to kill whoever broke into his house.

In Minnesota, we have a lot of people who deer hunt. In fact, we have a lot of deer hunters in Morrison County. I'm one of them. We hide in stands on or off the ground for hours waiting for a deer to come into our area so that we can kill it. We usually bring something to eat and drink because we know we are going to be sitting for long periods of time. Sitting still and quiet. After the kill, we drag the deer away from the scene, then go back and sit in the stand, waiting for the next kill.

Byron's deer stand was his basement reading chair, positioned between bookshelves to keep him hidden. He parked his pickup away from his house to make it look like no one was home. He had energy bars and bottles of water next to him for the long wait. He was reading a book so he could keep quiet until his prey came into sight. When his prey was near, he made the kill. After the kill, he dragged the prey away from the scene, reloaded his gun, and then sat back in his chair waiting for the next kill. Just like a deer hunter.

I was told our office received another call of a suspicious vehicle parked along Smith Avenue about one block east of Byron's driveway. The vehicle was a Mitsubishi Eclipse two-door hatchback with Minnesota license plates that were registered to Jason Brady. From previous contacts with Jason, we knew he was the father of Nicholas Brady. We now believed the unidentified body of the male victim located in Byron's residence was Nicholas, and that Nicholas drove to Byron's residence using that vehicle. Haile was probably the passenger in the vehicle. We had the vehicle towed to our secured storage garage so that a search warrant could be done on it.

Brian Middendorf and Todd Kosovich arrived at the sheriff's office and agreed to assist me and Agent Museus with drafting search warrants for Byron Smith's residence, the Mitsubishi Eclipse two-door hatchback registered to Jason Brady, the Chevy S-10 pickup truck registered to Byron Smith, the attached two-stall garage and the two-stall detached garage located at Byron's residence, and a quantity of blood which was to be removed from Byron Smith for further DNA analysis. Together, we drafted five separate search warrants.

After drafting the search warrants, I made phone contact with the on-call judge, the Honorable Jay Carlson. I faxed each search warrant to Judge Carlson for his review and approval. Judge Carlson called me for each individual warrant, and each time, I swore an oath to him that the facts outlined in the warrant were true and accurate to the best of my knowledge. I signed each search warrant and faxed them to him, and in return, he signed and approved each search warrant and then faxed them back to me.

My partner, Sergeant Investigator Jason Worlie, was called in to help with executing the search warrants. The plan was for BCA Agent Museus and his colleagues to go to Byron's house and start processing the crime scene. Jason and I were to meet with Byron in the jail and take him to the local hospital to obtain a sample of his blood. With each task assigned, we headed out.

Jason and I got to the jail at 9:00 p.m. and met with Byron. I served Byron a copy of the search warrant and told him we would be taking him to St. Gabriel's Hospital to obtain a quantity of his blood. Byron said he understood, and I placed handcuffs on him. We walked Byron out of the jail and down to our garage, where my squad car was parked. I had Byron take a seat in the back, and we transported him to the hospital, about eight blocks away from our office.

We arrived at the hospital at 9:05 p.m. and walked Byron into the ER. A sample of blood was drawn from Byron by a registered nurse using the BCA blood kit we provided. I asked Byron to initial the tags used to seal the vials of blood, and I then placed the seals on the vials. The blood kit was then sealed in Byron's presence. After I obtained the blood sample from Byron for evidence, we transported him back to the jail and turned him over to the on-duty correctional officers.

When that was completed, Jason and I drove to Byron's residence to meet with the BCA agents and assist with the search of the crime scene. Jason went into the house, and I gave Byron's blood sample to the BCA's mobile crime lab RV, which was parked in the driveway. I signed an evidence receipt stating that I released the blood sample to them to maintain a chain of evidence.

Maintaining a chain of evidence is very important. It's one of the first things a defense attorney will look at to try to get evidence thrown out. If proper procedures aren't followed, your evidence won't be permissible, and you can pretty much kiss your case goodbye. Defense attorneys will make the officer look inept on the stand if the officer did not do their job properly.

After turning over my evidence, I entered the house and

met with the BCA agents who were processing the scene. Agent Museus told me they moved the blood-stained rug at the bottom of the stairs. He said they found both blood and brain matter on the floor beneath the rug. I told Agent Museus that had to be the boy's blood and brain matter because Byron had shot him in the head when he was lying wounded at the bottom of the stairs.

"It appears Byron must have put the rug over the blood and brain matter after shooting the boy to cover it up," Agent Museus said.

I believed that Byron had covered up his kill prior to sitting back down in his chair. Otherwise, anyone else who began walking down the stairs would see the mess and turn around. If he had not covered it up, the girl probably wouldn't have continued down the stairs to become his second victim. Byron failed to tell me in his interview that he had done this.

Thinking back on it, I now realize that after following Byron down the stairs, I had stood on that rug for some time while he told me about his prior break-in and the shoes under his reading chair.

Agent Museus told me that they were able to positively identify the teenage victims. Deputy Rick Mattison, who assisted with the search warrant when the BCA agents arrived at the house, had recently had contact with both teens when he was investigating a suspicious vehicle complaint south of Little Falls. Mattison was able to identify the male victim as Nicholas Brady and the female victim was Nick's cousin, Haile Kifer.

Nick and Haile's bodies were placed in body bags and arrangements were made to have one of our deputies transport their bodies to the Ramsey County Medical Examiner's

Office for complete autopsies. The medical examiner details the cause of death by confirming how many times each victim had been shot, the location of each shot, and the shot(s) most likely to have resulted in death. The examiner also examines the angle of the shots and confirms the caliber of firearm that was used. Any bullets recovered from the bodies are turned over to the BCA to be matched with murder weapons. The BCA recovered the 14-mm rifle and the .22 caliber pistol from the upstairs entryway closets just off the kitchen.

Our department was very fortunate to have a chaplain. Chaplain Greg Valentine was to give the death notification to the families of Nicholas and Haile. He had to meet with them and tell them their children are dead. Many times, I had to tell family members and loved ones that the person they care most about in this world is dead. This information is never received well. Their reactions are heart-wrenching, and these meetings become memories that live on with you forever. It's a burden that comes with being a law enforcement officer, these moments that we carry through our jobs and long after our careers are over.

What helps me get by in these moments is the knowledge that I can help these families by doing my best to bring to justice the person who caused their loved one's death. That, and my strong faith in God and Jesus Christ. It's hard not to judge people for their actions, but I know my faith tells me not to. I try to hold out hope that no matter what bad things a person does in life, someday they will see the light and ask Jesus to forgive their sins. By making people answer for the wrongs they have done to others, I believe I'm following God's plan for me here on earth: to help bring people back into the light of God so that their souls don't slip away into the darkness of hell. I held hands with family members and the chaplain while he was giving last rites to the deceased.

Agent Museus told me of a disturbing discovery. Some of the light bulbs in the basement had been removed, particularly in the area where Byron was sitting. It appeared Byron removed these light bulbs so that if someone broke into the house and turned on the lights to walk down the stairs, they wouldn't see him sitting in his reading chair between the bookshelves.

Agent Museus told me they found a video surveillance recorder sitting on a table in the back-office room where the bodies had been lying. The surveillance recorder appeared to be working, and we hoped it would provide good evidence to help our case. However, we were not sure of how to get into the system to be able to watch the recording. I realized I'd have to attempt another statement with Byron to see if he would tell me how to retrieve the video surveillance recording. I also wanted to hear what he had to say about parking his truck a quarter mile away from his residence.

THE THIRD AND FINAL INTERVIEW

"I'm going back to the office to attempt a third statement from Byron to see if I can get the information we need," I told Agent Museus.

He agreed that was a good idea, and told me they'd continue with their work at the house. I left the residence and headed back to the sheriff's office. On the drive back, I was thinking about how Byron had the right to make a phone call while in custody. I hoped he hadn't yet contacted an attorney. My fear was that if he did talk to an attorney, they would probably advise him not to give any further statements to law enforcement. If that happened and Byron refused to talk with me, then there would be no way we could obtain the video surveillance recording.

If Byron had talked to an attorney, I could still attempt a statement from him, but I would have to be very careful about how I proceeded in getting the statement if Byron did not agree to talk with me. It would be very important that his statement make clear that he knows his legal rights, specifically that he has the right to have an attorney present with him while I'm talking with him, and that he is waiving that right of his own volition and has decided to talk with me without his attorney being present. Nothing is ever easy in my line of work.

I got back to the office at 12:50 a.m. I grabbed my digital recorder and immediately went up to the jail. There's a small room that we called the *intoxilyzer room*, which was located across the hallway from the booking room. We commonly used that room to interview people who were currently in jail. The room was mostly used for processing DUI suspects. It housed a desk and a couple of chairs. I radioed master control to have Byron brought over to the intoxilyzer room for our meeting.

One of the correctional officers brought Byron into the room a short time later, and I asked Byron to have a seat. I told Byron I had some further questions I would like to ask him, and I then turned on my digital audio recorder. I started my third statement with Byron.

Luberts: This is Sergeant Investigator Jeremy Luberts with the Morrison County Sheriff's Office, and the date is 11/24/2012 and the time right now is 12:58 a.m. I am currently in the intoxilyzer room at the Morrison County Jail and currently present with me is Byron Smith, and this will be a continuation, a follow-up interview with Byron.

Ok, now Byron, I had talked with you previously, you had been placed under arrest today.

Smith: Yep.

Luberts: Is that correct?

Smith: Yesterday, whatever.

Luberts: Yesterday actually, in fact it was yes, on the twenty-third. I had previously read you what's called the warning and consent form, those are your Miranda warning legal rights. Is that correct?

Smith: That's correct.

Luberts: Okay, would you like me, before I talk to you, to re-read you these Miranda warning rights?

Smith: I remember them from before, that's sufficient.

Luberts: Okay, so it's fair to say that you remember and understand your rights?

Smith: Yes.

Luberts: Okay, having these rights in mind are you willing to answer some more questions that I have for you?

Smith: I'm certainly willing to listen to the questions.

Luberts: Okay, did you get a chance to talk with an attorney?

Smith: Yes, I did. I talked with Greg on the phone and basically what he said was that things so far are going well enough.

Luberts: Okay, after, so you said you talked to an attorney, his name was Greg, on the phone, is that correct?

Smith: Yes.

Luberts: While you were up here in the jail?

Smith: Greg Larson, yes.

Luberts: Okay, and this was after I had initially talked to you the first time, correct?

Smith: Yes.

Luberts: Okay, and after speaking with your attorney are you okay with talking to me now without your attorney present, and answering further questions that I have for you?

Smith: Yes, I'm willing to talk with you even though he's not here now.

Luberts: Okay, and you do know that you do have the right to have him present with you at any time during any further questioning that I have. You understand that, right?

Smith: I understand that.

Luberts: And you're willing to waive that right to talk to me?

Smith: Answer some questions, yes, I waive that right, right now.

Luberts: Okay, and then Byron, I just have a few other questions for you in regard to this matter. First question I have for you is, you mentioned that you had a security camera video system set up at your house, correct?

Smith: It was a preliminary set up. I was still in the process of doing it, but the cameras have been running for the past week or more.

Luberts: Okay.

Smith: And there are four outdoor cameras placed around the house; because of my previous training in such matters, I believe in having a system that's concealed as well as practical. I'm not totally satisfied with the location of the cameras, but it's a good start.

Luberts: Okay, where were your cameras set up? You say they were all outside, is that correct?

Smith: I was monitoring two cameras on the basement door, one camera on the front living room door, and one camera looking at the approach to the main door from the driveway.

Luberts: Okay.

Smith: I have not yet got one installed looking directly at the door.

Luberts: Okay.

Smith: But it's, as I said, it will be an ongoing system for a long while.

Luberts: Okay, and these were out—these cameras were all outside, is that correct?

Smith: Yes, they were all outdoors.

Luberts: Okay, were there any cameras inside the house at all?

Smith: Not yet.

Luberts: Okay, okay.

Smith: Ah, right now I've got a four-channel machine hooked up, I'm going to swap it out for an eight-channel machine that I already have.

Luberts: Okay, the system you got set up, where's your monitor kept at?

Smith: The monitor is in the basement shop on the bench at the outside or south-side end of the shop.

Luberts: Okay, and that is the—when I say monitor, I'm referring to a TV monitor that projects what the cameras are showing.

Smith: Yeah, I have a rack mount set of three monitors, one of them is on—only one of them is hooked up because the digital video recorder only has a single monitor output.

Luberts: Okay.

Smith: If any single camera is important, it can be operated as an independent loop through but it's not switchable.

Luberts: Okay, so at the time this incident occurred at your house, when you said these two broke into your house.

Smith: Yes.

Luberts: How many cameras were recording do you think?

Smith: All of them.

Luberts: All of them.

Smith: Yes.

Luberts: So, all of your outside ones?

Smith: Mm-hmm.

Luberts: Okay.

Smith: The system has, maybe sixty-hour recycle time.

Luberts: Okay.

Smith: Which allows me to review it every other day to see what's happening.

Luberts: Okay.

Smith: And I have found mice in like, leaves. Squirrels running through and all that kind of stuff. It's got pretty good resolution.

Luberts: And it records onto you said, it's a—

Smith: It's a hard drive.

Luberts: So, it's digitally recorded.

Smith: Right.

Luberts: Okay, and then, to view this, is there a password or security code to get into this?

Smith: I've already offered to give that to anyone who wants to look at it, I consider it good verification and more accurate than the information I gave earlier.

Luberts: Okay, are you willing to share with me the security code?

Smith: Oh sure. It's the user password. In fact, I'll give you full instructions on how to pull the information out later. If you want to record them, we can or we can do it now.

Luberts: Why don't we go through it now if we can?

Smith: Okay.

Byron then went into details about how to access the surveillance system so we could watch and record the video for evidence.

Luberts: Now do you have a cell phone?

Smith: Yes, but it's currently not active because the time expired because I don't use it much.

Luberts: Okay, so what kind of cell phone is it? Is it a pre-paid?

Smith: I got it free as a leftover. When the project shut down, they didn't take in the old cell phones because they were old.

Luberts: Okay.

Smith: And, on a $460 million-dollar project, who cares about an out-of-date $20 cell phone?

Luberts: Okay.

Smith: So, they were abandoned, so I kept mine.

Luberts: When's the last time you used that cell phone?

Smith: I tried to turn it on about two months ago.

Luberts: Okay.

Smith: That's when I found out the time had expired.

Luberts: Okay.

Smith: In other words, I hadn't used any for so long that the time expired.

Luberts: Okay.

Smith: But the only place I am able to get it filled for free without buying a contract is at Mobile T-1.

Luberts: Okay, have you refilled this contract or been using it at all?

Smith: I'm afraid to make trips to St. Cloud because I'll get raided.

Luberts: Okay, okay.

Smith: I-I-I haven't left town; I haven't gone shopping.

Luberts: Okay.

Smith: I intended to, and I'm sure I will because it's a nice little phone.

Luberts: Mm-hmm.

Smith: It's smaller than your recorder.

Luberts: Okay, so it hasn't been functioning or working for, you figure, two months, or you turned it on two months ago?

Smith: Two months ago, it wasn't working. I don't know when it expired.

Luberts: Okay, so mostly you have been using the phone in your home, correct?

Smith: Right, the one in the kitchen.

Luberts: Okay, how many phones do you have in your house?

Smith: There are two that are plugged in, one in the kitchen, one down in the shop.

Luberts: Okay.

Smith: There are many phones in the house because I do electronics. I don't have the one in the bedroom plugged in because I don't like getting woken up when I'm sleeping.

Luberts: Okay, alright, and the bedroom you're referring to where you don't want to get woken up—

Smith: Is my bedroom, the corner bedroom.

Luberts: Is that ah, where is that located in the house, upstairs, downstairs, or where?

Smith: It's the northwest corner on the main floor.

Luberts: Okay.

Smith: And also, it's built as a retirement home, everything necessary is on the main floor.

Luberts: Okay, alright, and the bedroom you showed me that the window was broken.

Smith: That's my bedroom.

Luberts: Is that the one—

Smith: Yes.

Luberts: The bedroom you're referring to that you sleep in?

Smith: Yes.

Luberts: Okay, okay.

Smith: I don't dare anymore because I'm afraid that Mr. Williams, who occasionally does crazy things when he gets drunk, will come and shoot me in my sleep some night.

Luberts: Okay.

Smith: I'm very worried about that.

Luberts: Okay, how many vehicles do you own, Byron?

Smith: That's a complicated question because I don't use all of them. See, I have a silver Chevy S-10 pick-up, and I have a Cayenne, those are the two vehicles I keep in the garage. I only use the Cayenne for road trips, it's not a grocery car, and it's a heavy car. I inherited a maroon Oldsmobile Cutlass 90–94, I think, from my mom, and currently I'm just keeping it because it only has sixteen thousand miles and is in extremely good condition. I have a—I also have a '69 Chevy Nova that was running, but a tree fell on it and restoration is on hold for lack of time.

Luberts: Okay. To clarify with you, how many pickup trucks do you own?

Smith: One.

Luberts: One, and what kind of pickup truck is that?

Smith: A silver Chevy S-10, '95.

Luberts: Okay, where is that pickup currently parked at?

Smith: It's parked in a cul-de-sac north of my other property, which is the adjacent property to the north.

Luberts: Um, this other property, do you remember what road, or, where the truck is parked that you said. Do you remember what road that is? You know the name of the road?

Smith: No, I don't.

Luberts: Okay, how far from your residence that you live at is it parked?

Smith: Three-minute walk.

Luberts: About a three-minute walk, okay, so are we talking, like ah, how many blocks do you think? How many blocks away?

Smith: One.

Luberts: How many?

Smith: One.

Luberts: One block, okay, so fairly close. Why do you have that vehicle parked over there?

Smith: I needed to clean out the garage and I wanted it out of the way for a while.

Luberts: Okay.

Smith: It's ah, time of the year to clean out the garage before it gets too cold to do it.

Luberts: Okay, and you said, is that where you have the—where you had the truck parked, is it in front of some property that you own there?

Smith: No, no it's out of the way, out of sight. I didn't want it vandalized.

Luberts: Okay, when did you park that truck there?

Smith: Ah, let's see, I was starting cleanup, that would have been Thursday morning.

Luberts: So, Thursday morning you said you parked it there?

Smith: Um, oh no, that would have been the trigger for them coming to see me. That would have been the trigger. That's why they came. They thought I had gone away.

Luberts: Okay.

Smith: They saw me drive the truck and they didn't see me come back because I walked back, and that's why they came.

Luberts: Okay. So, you drove the truck out of your residence that morning, Thursday morning you said, correct?

Smith: Yeah, ah, yeah.

Luberts: Which is Thanksgiving morning?

Smith: Yeah, right.

Luberts: Okay, and then you drove it over to this cul-de-sac, which I believe is Oak Lane, does that sound accurate to you?

Smith: There is an Oak Lane there, yeah.

Luberts: Okay, was this Oak Lane that you parked your truck alongside the road on?

Smith: Yes.

Luberts: Okay, and what time did you go and move your vehicle and park it there? Do you remember?

Smith: Ah, mid-morning.

Luberts: Mid-morning.

Smith: Yeah, mid-morning.

Luberts: Can you give me a rough idea about what time that would be?

Smith: I'm guessing a little after 11:00.

Luberts: A little after 11:00?

Smith: Yeah, that should be on the videotape.

Luberts: Okay.

Smith: You could get the exact time.

Luberts: Okay, okay, so you parked it over there and then you walked back to your house?

Smith: Yeah, uh-huh.

Luberts: Do you own property off of Oak Lane?

Smith: No.

Luberts: Okay.

Smith: No, I just wanted it out of the way because I keep my garages locked. I'm worried about vandalism.

Luberts: Okay, have you ever parked your vehicle over there before?

Smith: No, I haven't.

Luberts: Prior to this day?

Smith: No.

Luberts: No, you haven't? What made you do— what made you want to park it over there on Thanksgiving?

Smith: Out of sight, out of the way. Because I wanted it out of the garage but I'm not leaving anything out where anybody can get to it.

Luberts: But wouldn't you be afraid somebody would come and break into it while it's parked along the road there?

Smith: They're not being raided over there. I'm being raided.

Luberts: Okay, I'm just asking.

Smith: Yeah—yeah, if it's out of sight it's, well, the property adjacent to mine was raided at the same time as the last break in. They kicked in the garage door; they kicked in the basement door.

Luberts: Okay.

Smith: So, I couldn't even park it there.

Luberts: Okay, there was what appeared to be possibly blood in the box or on the vehicle. Can you tell me where that would have come from?

Smith: Ah, trying to remember. You would have to check to see it was—if it was human blood or beaver blood.

Luberts: Okay.

Smith: Ah, I did carry the beaver there but there wouldn't have been very much.

Luberts: Okay, did you ever like, throw beaver that you had in the box of the pickup or anywhere in the pickup?

Smith: Yeah, it's, or it—I –I—that section of property is still quite wild. There's a varmint problem too.

Luberts: Okay.

Smith: So, if it's more than a month old it could have been coyote blood, or, it could have been muskrat blood.

Luberts: Okay, you mentioned it might have also been human blood. Can you tell me why?

Smith: Yeah, I was dripping. I was dripping all over the place. You'll find big pools of my blood on the floor in the basement.

Luberts: You pointed and referred to that and I see you got a scab on the top of your head.

Smith: Yeah.

Luberts: Is that because—you're saying that because, if you had an injury to the top of your head, that would have caused the blood?

Smith: Yeah, in fact, specifically, it'd be a week and a half ago now, I was carrying a box up the stairs and near the top of the stairs I overbalanced backwards.

Luberts: Okay.

Smith: And I still feel like I've been given a massage with a pair of tire irons and when I slid down the stairs headfirst, of course, it was my head that struck at the bottom.

Luberts: Okay, okay.

Smith: And I was dripping off and on throughout the day, so, it might be mine.

Luberts: Okay.

Smith: There is no reason whatsoever though that it would be either the male or the female that were in the basement.

Luberts: Okay, okay, alright. Byron, I—

Smith: I now realize why they came while I was there.

Luberts: Why is that? Why you—

Smith: Because they thought I was gone.

Luberts: Okay, because of you parking your truck over.

Smith: Yeah, I moved the truck out of vandalism range and so they assumed that I was gone.

Luberts: Did you have any other vehicles parked out in your yard after you moved the truck?

Smith: No, I have in the past couple weeks. I had two out of the garage, but I moved them into the three-car garage on the adjacent property.

Luberts: Okay.

Smith: Because I'm hiding everything.

Luberts: Okay, that pickup of yours, do you typically leave that parked outside when you're home?

Smith: I have about half the time during this past summer, yes.

Luberts: Okay.

Smith: Depending upon where things are, what I'm doing, I might park it behind the cedar trees, or in the driveway if I'm going back and forth for things. I use the truck as a work vehicle in the yard. I hauled the trailer with it.

Luberts: Okay, okay, Byron that's all the questions I have at this point, so.

Smith: I'm—I'm shocked I didn't ever realize that.

Luberts: Okay, Byron, this concludes this statement then and the time is 1:19 a.m.

After finishing my statement with Byron, I walked him back over to the booking room and turned him over to the correctional officers. I left the jail and drove back over to Byron's residence.

When I got back to the residence, I met with Agent Museus and told him what I had discovered. He was glad I was able to get the instructions on how to access and retrieve the video from Byron's surveillance recorder. He was also amazed that Byron agreed to give me another statement after I told him that he had talked with an attorney prior to me getting back to the jail to talk with him. The first thing a lawyer will usually tell their client is to not give any statements to the police.

This is why I treat everyone with kindness, understanding, and respect, no matter what they have done in their lives. I truly believe that if I had been judgmental of or rude or mean to Byron in any way, he probably would have shut down and declined to talk with me any further. It pays to kill them with kindness.

We were getting close to finishing up with the search warrant of the residence and the BCA agents were going to take the evidence found there so it could be processed in their lab.

I was taking one last look around the basement and was standing in the office room that the bodies had been found in. I saw a small handheld digital audio recorder sitting on top of a desk. I grabbed the recorder and turned it on, but the batteries were dead. I showed the recorder to Agent Museus.

"We found the same type of recorder sitting on top of books in the bookshelf above the reading chair that Byron had been sitting in near the bottom of the stairs. We checked that recorder also and the batteries are dead."

"Are you planning on taking the recorders as evidence to see if there is anything on them?" I asked.

"No, the batteries are dead, and it looks like they haven't been used in a long time."

"I want you to take both recorders and have them analyzed to see if there is anything on them."

He argued with me that it would be a waste of time because it was obvious to them that they hadn't been used in a long time.

Byron told me that he had worked for the State Department installing surveillance systems in embassies. I had a strong gut feeling that there might be something recorded on one of these digital recorders that could help the case. I wasn't taking no for an answer.

"I want these recorders analyzed, and if you're not willing to take them, I will have them analyzed myself!" Agent Museus could see that I was very serious about this and reluctantly agreed to take the recorders and have them analyzed.

I then finished my final look around the residence. The assisting officers, BCA agents, and I searched the attached garage and the detached garage. No items of evidence were found in the garages. On the kitchen table, we left a copy of the search warrant along with an evidence receipt of everything we took from the residence. We locked all the doors to the residence, making sure it was secure. We then cleared from the residence at 3:57 a.m. and drove back to the sheriff's office.

CHAPTER
11

BACK HOME

We got back to the office at 4:05 a.m. and met in our conference room. One of our officers thought that we should have the BCA agents reinterview Byron. I quickly spoke up. "That's not going to happen! Have you even watched or heard the statements I took from him?"

The officer said he hadn't.

"Then why would you want the BCA to reinterview him?"

"Because they probably have more experience than you do at it."

"I know what the hell I'm doing!"

Agent Museus looked at the officer and said, "Jeremy did a great job with the interviews, and I don't see any need for any of us to reinterview Byron or get in the way of Jeremy's progress."

I gave the officer a stern look, then turned away. I wanted to tell him to shut his pie hole when he doesn't know what he's talking about, but I reserved myself from saying anything. Sometimes, certain people just can't help themselves from being a dick.

It had been a very long day and we were all crabby and exhausted. We decided it was time for a break and that everyone should go home and get a little sleep. We decided to meet back up at the office at 10:00 a.m. to continue with the investigation. The BCA agents left and went to one of our local hotels. I left the office and went home.

I finally got home at 4:50 a.m. My duty belt and bulletproof vest felt like a hundred pounds by then. I couldn't wait to take them off. I slipped my boots off, then tiptoed into the bedroom, trying not to wake my wife. I took off my duty belt, bulletproof vest, and uniform and hung everything in the closet. I walked into my daughter's bedroom next door to ours and gave her a kiss on the forehead. She looked like a little angel to me, sleeping so quietly and cuddled in her blanket.

My eyes started to tear up a little as I was standing there looking at her. I couldn't help but think how glad I was that my daughter was at home, safe and sound. Someone else's daughter would never return home again.

I walked back into my bedroom and crawled into bed. My wife was sound asleep, snoring. I closed my eyes, hoping to finally pass out from exhaustion. My mind was racing with thoughts of everything I'd seen that day and everything I had left to do. I started to doze off, and suddenly I saw a flashback of Nick and Haile's bodies lying dead on the floor. Then, all of a sudden, I could smell their dead bodies.

I opened my eyes and lay in bed for a little while, hoping my mind would shut down. I wanted to close my eyes because my eyelids felt very heavy, but I was afraid to because of the images I'd just seen.

I lay there looking into the dark, trying my best to picture a bright light. A light that would grow all through my body with a warm feeling of comfort and joy. I was doing my best to enlighten my spirit to help bring me peace. With God's grace and love for me, it worked. I was finally able to fall asleep.

My alarm clock went off at 8:00 a.m. and it felt like I had just fallen asleep. I slept for about two hours. I felt like a zombie and probably looked like one too. I'm a smoker, so my mouth tasted like an ashtray. My eyes felt like they were on fire from lack of rest, and my head was pounding. I said to myself, oh, this is going to be a lovely day!

Chrissy and Hailey were up. I could hear them in the dining room. I walked into the dining room and Chrissy asked me how my day went and what happened.

"Two teenagers were killed, but I can't talk about it." The truth was, I didn't want to talk about it. "How are you feeling?"

"Not good." She was still feeling very weak and was having bad stomach cramps. She still looked very pale to me, almost white as a ghost.

Chrissy looked at me, again, with that unnerving look, and asked me, "Do you have to go back into work today?"

Oh boy! I knew what was coming next, but I had no choice but to tell her. "Yes, I have to get ready and be back to the office in an hour." She didn't look pale to me anymore; her face turned beet-red and her eyes flashed. The words she spoke next are against my religion to repeat. It was not good. I didn't blame Chrissy for being upset. I tried to explain to her that I really didn't have a choice in the matter, but it was to no avail. Everything I said made things worse. The only words she wanted to hear come out of my mouth were *I'll be home*. I wanted nothing more in the world than to stay home that day, but I had to work.

"I'm sorry, honey." I turned away and walked into the bathroom to get ready for work. I could still hear her mumbling and grumbling through the closed bathroom door. I jumped into the shower, brushed my teeth, brushed on some deodorant, then headed to the bedroom to put on my uniform. My daughter, Hailey, came into the bedroom and asked, "Daddy, why is Mommy so upset with you? Will you make me some pancakes for breakfast?"

"Sorry, Hailey, I can't make you pancakes this morning. Daddy's got to go back to work. Mommy is mad at Daddy because I won't be home with you today."

"Then I'm mad at you too, Daddy!" She walked out of the bedroom, and I continued to get ready for work. I was hurting inside because the most important people in my life were both mad at me, but I also had to chuckle. It was amazing how those two stuck together.

I finished getting ready for work. I walked past Chrissy and Hailey in the dining room.

"See you as soon as I can. Love you both." I was met with complete silence, which was never a good sign. I walked out of the house and had a seat in my squad car.

The temperature outside was twelve degrees. The seat in my Chevy Tahoe felt like sitting on a frozen brick. I started my engine and waited for it to warm up. While I was sitting there, I thought back to a time when I left an unopen can of diet Dr. Pepper in the center console of my squad car in the middle of the winter. The temperature had dropped below zero and the next morning when I walked out to start my squad, it looked like a bomb had gone off in my vehicle. There was frozen pop everywhere. All over the ceiling, windshield, dash, seats, steering wheel, and my radio equipment. The aluminum can was blown apart at the top. I couldn't believe what had happened. I had no idea that a frozen pop can would do that. Needless to say, I never left an unopen pop can in my vehicle again.

After fifteen minutes of shivering, my squad finally warmed up. I radioed to my dispatch, "106, 800, I'll be in service." I logged into my computer, then drove to the sheriff's office.

SEARCH WARRANTS OF THE VEHICLES

It was Saturday, November 24, 2012. I arrived at the office at 9:00 a.m. I didn't need to be there until ten, but I was always early for work. Ever since I started as a cop seventeen years ago, I had always made sure to be at least half an hour early to work. I thank my dad for instilling a hard work ethic in me when I was growing up.

I made a pot of coffee and waited for the BCA agents to arrive. And no, I didn't have doughnuts. Not all cops eat doughnuts. I have no idea who started that rumor, but it is not true. At least not for me.

The BCA agents arrived at ten and we met in our conference room to go over the case and plan out our day. One of the officers brought in a box of doughnuts to share with everyone. The irony is not lost on me. Way to prove me wrong, fellow officer.

We still had two search warrants left to complete: the search warrant on the Eclipse two-door hatchback registered to Jason Brady, and the warrant on the 1995 Chevy S-10 pickup registered to Byron Smith.

At 2:01 p.m., one of the BCA agents and I went to our county storage garage and executed the search warrant on the Eclipse two-door hatchback. I took pictures of the outside and inside of the car. Then we put on rubber gloves, not knowing what kind of nasty things we might find inside.

In the glovebox we found a driver's license application receipt with the name *Haile Kifer* on it. On the back seat, we found a paper from one of our local schools that appeared to be a class schedule. It had the name *Nicholas Brady* on it. We then knew that Nicholas and Haile had been in that vehicle, and we could confirm that this was the vehicle they had driven the day they parked a block away from Byron Smith's residence.

I was digging through stuff on the floor behind the driver's seat and found a small black Calvin Klein bag. The bag was zipped closed. I opened it to see what was inside, and laughed at the contents. Inside, there was a black dildo and a string of black anal beads. After the surprise wore off, I wondered why these kids had sex toys in their car. I figured they probably stole them from someone. I was grateful for my rubber gloves.

I remember a time back before Michel was sheriff. He was the patrol sergeant, and I was a road deputy. We were helping the drug task force do a drug search warrant at a house. I was standing in the hallway of the house, talking with another officer and suddenly, I felt something poking me in the left cheek. I turned my head to the left and saw the head of a big pink dildo staring me in the face! Other officers in the house saw what happened and started laughing their asses off! I started rubbing my left cheek frantically with the disgusting thought of what germs could have been on that thing that were now on my face. I couldn't help but laugh when I told Michel, "You asshole! I'll get you back!" Officers love playing jokes on each other. It helps us deal with the traumatic things we experience in our job.

Lying on the back seat, I found six prescription pill bottles that had the name of one of our local retired schoolteachers on the bottles. I'm not going to disclose the name of the teacher, but I will say it was a male teacher. I could not think of any reason why those pill bottles would be in this vehicle unless the kids had stolen them.

Inside the car, we also found a Louisville Slugger wooden bat with a signature on it, a Kodak digital camera, a hand-crank flashlight, a hedge clipper with the name "Tony" written on the handle, collectible coins and bills including foreign money, a red box with jewelry inside, a two-dollar bill in a plastic sleeve, and a gold-colored men's Pulsar watch. I'm guessing some of the items might also have been stolen from the teacher's residence.

I took pictures of all the items as they were found in the car. I collected the items for evidence by putting the items in evidence bags. Then I placed them in my squad car. I filled out an evidence receipt form and placed a copy of the form along with a copy of the search warrant on the driver's seat. This completed our search warrant for the car.

At 3:42 p.m., we moved to Byron Smith's vehicle, the 1995 Chevy S-10 pickup, to execute that search warrant. I started by taking pictures of the outside and inside of the pickup. We then searched the truck. We didn't find any items of interest, so no items of evidence were seized from the truck. I filled out an evidence receipt form and noted that no items of evidence were taken from the truck. I then left a copy of the evidence receipt form and a copy of the search warrant on the driver's seat. This completed our search warrant on the truck.

It was no surprise to me that we didn't find any items of evidentiary value in Byron's pickup. The main evidence regarding Byron's pickup was that he had parked it away from his residence to make it look like he wasn't home.

After completing the search warrants on the vehicles, we drove back to the sheriff's office. On my computer, I logged all the evidence I collected during the search warrants. I then secured the evidence in my evidence locker.

I took my digital camera and downloaded all the pictures I had taken so far so that they could be added to the case file.

While I was busy at the office, my partner and one of the BCA agents went to talk with neighbors that lived near Byron's residence. They obtained a statement from Kathleen Lange, who said she had lived in the neighborhood for twenty years and was very familiar with people in the area and their vehicles.

Kathleen stated she noticed a small red car, which was later determined to be the vehicle Nicholas Brady and Haile Kifer were in, parked on Smith Avenue. She said she noticed the car there on Friday, November 23 around 2:00 p.m. when she went to town. She said no one was around the car and she was wondering which house it belonged to because it was not parked near a residence.

Next, they obtained a statement from her husband, John Lange. John stated that around 2:00 p.m. on Thanksgiving Day he heard a single shot that sounded muffled. He said he didn't think much of it because he knows Byron Smith usually shoots at beavers in the area.

John said he noticed the red car parked on Smith Avenue

but was not sure when it arrived.

John stated he knew Byron Smith well, and had talked to him on Wednesday, November 21. John said he invited Byron to Thanksgiving because he knew Byron didn't have any family in the area. He said Byron declined and told him he was going out of town.

John said Byron had told him he wasn't feeling well because he slipped and fell in his residence and had a cut on his head. He said he invited Byron to go with him to Pierz on Wednesday, but Byron declined because he wasn't feeling well.

John said he also spoke with William Anderson, who is also friends with Byron. William told him that Byron had been acting weird lately, and that William believed he may have a concussion from falling at his residence.

John stated it is well-known in the neighborhood not to mess with Byron, and that he and Anderson are the only two who visit Byron.

Byron's brother, Bruce Smith, called the sheriff's office and asked if he could come in and talk with a deputy. Bruce was asked to come in at around 6:00 p.m.

Bruce arrived at the sheriff's office on time and met with Sergeant Worlie and one of the BCA agents in the interview room. Bruce agreed to give the officers a recorded statement.

In his statement, Bruce said on Thursday, November 22, he received a phone call from his brother, Byron. Byron stated he couldn't talk about anything over the phone because it was not a secure situation, but he then asked Bruce how soon Bruce could get to his residence. Bruce said he was in Pennsylvania but would check the flight loads and get there as soon as possible.

Bruce said he had no idea what was going on, but he

could tell it was something serious, so he rushed to get back to Little Falls as soon as possible. Bruce said he had talked with Byron recently, and he knew Byron was concerned about security issues at his house because of previous break-ins. He said Byron told him he was in the process of upgrading surveillance cameras at his residence.

Bruce said that as far as he knows, Byron is healthy, both mentally and physically. Bruce stated that Byron sounded distraught on the phone when he called him on Thursday.

Bruce said it almost seemed like Byron didn't know what to do. He said Byron had held a high-security job and recently retired, but he didn't have any experience with weapons or war of any kind.

Bruce said that during that call, Byron had mentioned the previous burglary where some guns and approximately $10,000 worth of stuff were taken. Bruce said Byron was very concerned and didn't feel safe in his own home.

We finally finished everything we needed to accomplish that day. It was 8:00 p.m. and the BCA agents were leaving to go back home. I had a ton of paperwork that I needed to get caught up on, so I stayed at the office until 11:00 p.m., then finally called it a day when I couldn't stand looking at the computer screen, filling out forms anymore. I had hardly put a dent in what I still needed to get done, but at least I was a little closer.

I got home at about 11:05 p.m. I stumbled into the house, happy to finally be home. I poked my head into Hailey's room to check on her, and she was sound asleep in her bed. I walked into my bedroom and Chrissy was sound asleep, snoring again. After taking my uniform and equipment off, which is like instantly shedding twenty-five pounds, I crawled into bed and passed out from exhaustion.

TRAGEDY AT HOME

It was Sunday, November 25, 2012. I woke up around 10:00 a.m. and was planning on relaxing and enjoying the day with my family. I knew Monday was going to be hectic at work, so I needed Sunday to relax and let my nerves calm down.

I crawled out of bed and got dressed for the day. Chrissy was in the bathroom and Hailey was watching TV in the living room. I went into the living room and greeted her.

"Good morning, sunshine."

"Daddy, do you have to go back into work today?"

"No, we have the whole day together." I was happy to be able to tell her that. She gave me a hug, then a kiss on the cheek.

"Good morning, honey," I said to Chrissy when she emerged from the bathroom. She looked terrible. She was still white as a ghost, but now, she was also having a hard time standing. I asked her what was wrong and she said she felt very weak and had been passing blood in her stool for the past couple of days.

"I think I have a GI bleed," she said, "and I feel like passing out."

"This could be serious; I'm going to bring you to the hospital." She didn't argue with me; she agreed she needed to go. I held her arm and helped her into the kitchen. I told Hailey to put on her coat and shoes. Chrissy was standing by the door, and I went to get her coat and shoes for her. When I got back to help her put her shoes on, Chrissy had collapsed onto the floor and was unconscious.

I was horrified. My whole body was shaking with adrenaline. I quickly checked to make sure she was still breathing, and thankfully she was. I grabbed my cell phone from its holder on my belt and tried to call 911 for an ambulance. For the life of me, I couldn't get my fingers to work well enough to even dial the numbers. I was shaking so badly, I could hardly hold onto the phone.

I took a couple of deep breaths and exhaled slowly, calming down just enough to dial the numbers. All 911 calls ring into our sheriff's office dispatch center. Jane Fussy was dispatching and answered the 911 call.

"Jane, this is 106, my wife just passed out and I need an ambulance right away."

Jane asked me where I was and I told her, "I'm at home, just send me an ambulance right now!"

"Jeremy, calm down, I'm going to send one right away. How is your wife doing?"

"I'm sorry for being upset, just please get the ambulance here. She's still unconscious." "It's going to be okay; the ambulance will be there shortly."

Ten minutes later, I could hear sirens coming down my street, getting closer to my house.

"Just hang on," I repeated to Chrissy, "help is coming." She was still unconscious but breathing. I just sat there, holding her in my arms until the ambulance arrived.

Suddenly, I heard crying behind me. I looked back and saw Hailey there with her coat and shoes on. She had big tears running down her cheeks, and her little body was shaking from crying so hard. All I could do was tell her, "Don't worry, Hailey, Mommy's going to be fine." I was trying to be a rock for her on the outside, but inside I was crumbling apart too.

There was a knock at the door and I told them to come in. One of the medics lived across the alley from me. I told them what happened and that we needed to get my wife to the hospital right away. I helped carry Chrissy out of the house and put her on the gurney. I then helped the medics get her loaded into the ambulance and they left for St. Gabriel's Hospital with their lights and siren on.

I'm a certified first responder, and in my career I have helped many people with medical emergencies. I have saved some people and watched others die. I've come to learn that nothing can prepare you to deal with a family member's medical emergency. I felt like my body was shutting down, and I couldn't even function properly.

I went back into the house and Hailey was still standing in the kitchen crying. I hugged her. "It's going to be fine, let's go be with Mommy." It was all I could do to fight back tears at that point. I had been taught that men are not supposed to cry, no matter how bad things got, and that's what I repeated to myself in those moments.

I was holding Hailey in my arms and headed out the door. I put Hailey in my truck, and we drove to the hospital. The hospital was only ten blocks away from my house, so we got there quickly.

I walked into the emergency room and saw the doctor and nurses helping my wife. She had an oxygen mask on her face and an IV in her arm. The doctor told me they ran a blood test and discovered that Chrissy's hemoglobin was very low, which is why she passed out. The doctor told me she must have lost a lot of blood over those past few days. He was not yet sure what was causing the blood loss, so they were taking her by ambulance to the St. Cloud Hospital for further testing. The St. Cloud Hospital is about thirty miles south of Little Falls. It is a much larger hospital and has a trauma unit.

I was holding onto Hailey's hand as she was staring at her mom lying on that hospital bed in the emergency room, the doctor and nurses surrounding her.

"Daddy, what are they doing to Mommy?"

"The doctor and nurses are trying to make Mommy better."

"Can I go hold Mommy's hand?"

"No, honey, you can't right now, but you can hold Daddy's hand as long as you want."

The medics came into the room to get Chrissy ready to be transported to the St. Cloud Hospital. I walked out into the waiting room and called Chrissy's parents to let them know what was going on. I then called my parents and my brother Jamie. Jamie and his wife, Jennifer, live next door to me. Jamie said they'd heard the siren and seen the flashing lights at our house and were wondering what was going on.

Hailey and I walked back to my truck. It's about a thirty-minute drive to the other hospital.

"Do you want to pray with Daddy for Mommy to get better?"

"Yes, do you think God is listening?"

"God always listens to our prayers. Of course he's listening, Sweetie." We made the sign of the cross, crossed our fingers and started to pray.

When we finished our prayers, Hailey said, "I know Mommy's going to be better now. God will hear us and take care of her."

"Hailey, you are so much like your Daddy," I told her.

We got to the St. Cloud Hospital and walked into the emergency room. There was a security guard and metal detector at the door. I told him I'm an officer and showed him my badge because I had my off-duty weapon concealed in a holster under my jacket. He asked me what department I worked for, and I told him I was at the Morrison County Sheriff's Office. He asked me if I knew anything about the two teenagers that had recently been killed, and I told him I was the arresting officer.

He looked at me and said, "I wouldn't want your job."

We walked over to the cubicle that Chrissy was in. She was lying down on the hospital bed with an IV in her arm. I was relieved to see she was awake.

"What happened?"

"You almost gave me a heart attack. You passed out at home, and I had to call an ambulance." I must have sounded a little dramatic because she started to laugh.

Chrissy said, "The doctor wants to put a scope down my throat and into my stomach to find out where I'm bleeding from."

"That sounds like a good idea. Hopefully they can figure something out."

We sat in the emergency room for two hours until Chrissy was finally moved into her own private room. Hailey lay in bed next to her mom while I sat in a chair beside them, holding Chrissy's hand. An hour went by and the nurses finally came into the room to say they were ready for Chrissy to have her procedure done. Chrissy was placed in a wheelchair and the nurses took her away. As she was leaving, I wished her good luck, and told her we'd be right there when she got back.

By this time, Hailey and I were starving because we hadn't eaten yet that day. I asked Hailey if she wanted to go down to the cafeteria with me to get something to eat. Her little eyes got wide, and she said, "Can I get some chicken strips and ice cream?" Hailey and I took the elevator down to the cafeteria and got our food.

We sat in a booth, ate, and talked for an hour. Christmas was only a month away, so I got ideas from her about what she wanted from Santa.

A couple of years before, I'd teased Hailey that she was going to get reindeer poop in her stocking from Santa because she'd been naughty. I took her with me to the Fleet Supply store before Christmas and the female clerk asked Hailey what she was getting from Santa. Hailey said, "Daddy told me I'm getting reindeer poop from Santa." I couldn't believe Hailey had outed me like that. The clerk looked at me in disbelief. I just stood there in shock. The clerk gave me a dirty look with my change.

All I could think to say was, "Kids say the funniest things, don't they?" Then we left the store. I learned a valuable lesson: don't ever say something to a child that you don't want repeated to an adult.

When Hailey and I finished eating, we went back to Chrissy's room. An hour had passed, and she wasn't back yet. We turned on the TV in the room to pass the time. There were multiple Christmas shows to choose from. That always cheers us up.

Another hour went by, and Chrissy still wasn't back. I was getting very worried. A little while later, the door opened, and Chrissy was brought back into the room. I asked her what happened.

"The doctor told me I have an ulcer in my stomach that was bleeding badly. That's why I lost so much blood. They were able to stop the bleeding, but I'm going to have to stay in the hospital for at least a couple of days. They have to monitor me to make sure the bleeding stopped and fill me back up with blood until my hemoglobin levels are normal." A tear rolled down her cheek as she was telling me this. I leaned over and gave her a kiss on the forehead.

"You're going to take off work and stay with me, right?" Anytime Chrissy had to stay in the hospital for anything, I always took off work and spent as much time with her as I could. I would even spend the night with her in the room. But this time was different.

"Honey, I can't. I'm right in the middle of this double murder case. The suspect is in custody, and I need to have my reports done by tomorrow because he has to be seen in court on his two murder charges."

More tears rolled down her cheeks. I could tell she was upset and had every right to be. "So, you're telling me your job is more important than your family?"

My heart sank when I heard those words. I had no answer for her. It was bad enough that I couldn't be at home to take care of her when she wasn't feeling good; now I couldn't even stay at the hospital with her. Damn this job sometimes! I got a feeling that one day, I'd lose my family because of this job. I hoped and prayed that wouldn't happen. I've come to realize that it takes a very special woman to be an investigator's wife. But I also know that everyone has their breaking point.

Visiting hours at the hospital ended at 8:00 p.m. I stayed at the hospital as long as I could. I was able to talk the nurse into letting Hailey and I stay until 9:00 p.m. When our visiting time expired, I told Chrissy, "I better take Hailey home so she can go to bed. She has school tomorrow. I'll be back tomorrow as soon as I get off work. I love you!"

She looked at me and said, "I won't hold my breath. You'll probably end up working all day and night again. Have a good night and drive safe." Hailey and I gave her a kiss, then we left the hospital.

Hailey fell asleep as soon as I got her in the truck. It was a miserable half-hour drive home. All I could think about was wanting to be with Chrissy. I hated the thought of having to sleep alone without her.

THE FIRST COURT APPEARANCE

Monday, November 26, 2012. My cell phone alarm was blaring. If cell phones weren't so expensive, I would have smashed it. I looked at the time and it was 6:00 a.m. I'd had a miserable night. The bed felt empty, and I couldn't fall asleep without my wife snoring in my ear. I had tossed and turned half the night. No matter what I did, I could not fall asleep. I heard long ago that drinking a glass of warm milk before bed was supposed to send a person off to sleep. I was desperate to try anything. I had gotten out of bed and heated up a glass. I took a big gulp, hoping the old remedy would work. To my surprise, it tasted horrible. I had no idea warm milk could taste so bad. How the hell can anyone drink warm milk?

I brushed my teeth to get the nasty taste out of my mouth and lay back down in bed. I finally fell asleep around 2:00 a.m.

At six o'clock, I crawled out of bed and got ready for work. After a hot shower and a cup of coffee, I was ready to tackle the day. My shift started at 7:00 a.m. and I got off work at 5:00 p.m. I still had to wake Hailey and get her ready for school, so I had to hustle. The school was only two blocks from my house, so I didn't have far to go to drop her off.

After getting Hailey ready, feeding her breakfast, and starting my squad car so we had a warm vehicle to get into, we headed out the door. I dropped Hailey off at school, then drove to our sheriff's office five blocks away.

I walked into my office and fired up the computer. I was not looking forward to the mound of paperwork and reports I had to get done that day. We dictated our reports into a digital recorder, then downloaded them into the computer for the administrative staff to type.

When I first started as a deputy, learning how to dictate a report was not easy. I was used to typing or writing everything down. At first, I would handwrite the report to make sure I had everything right and then dictate it. It would take me double the time. After a couple of months of doing that, I was finally able to dictate my reports. I just had to remember to keep everything in chronological order. Now, after seventeen years on the job, it just comes naturally.

I liked to listen to the statements I'd taken with suspects before I added them to my report. That way everything was very accurate. It's important that an officer add every detail they can think of into their reports. If the information is not in the report, then in the defense attorney's eyes, it basically didn't happen.

I've seen lots of officers try to add details during their testimonies that were not in their original reports. That's a big mistake. When that happens, defense attorneys jump all over the officers. They say things like, "Officer, why wasn't this information in your report?" and that's a bad misstep to have to explain to a judge and jury. It makes them wonder if the information was missing because you were trying to hide something.

My report was so detailed, it took me three hours to complete. Getting it done was a big relief. After the administrative staff typed the report, I reviewed it once again to catch any corrections that would need to be made before it could be sent to the county attorney to bring criminal charges against Byron Smith.

There was a lot more follow-up for me to do in this case, and there would be plenty more supplemental reports to follow. But for now, my biggest concern of having the initial report completed for the criminal charges was over.

Working a big case brings great responsibility and stress. Not only did I have the sheriff and chief deputy watching my every move, but I also had the other deputies, county attorney's office, defense attorney, judge, general public, and news media watching as well. Most people think it's glamorous to be an investigator, but it's not. If only it was as glamorous as TV makes it out to be . . .

The news media caught wind of Byron's arrest over the weekend and that morning, it was all over the TV and newspapers. Phone calls had been streaming into our office from news outlets looking for information. News media vans were already lined up down Elm Street in front of Byron's driveway.

I gathered all the search warrants we executed along with the evidence receipts from the scenes. I had ten days to file the paperwork with the court after the search warrant was issued by the judge. I walked upstairs to the court administration's office to file the warrants ahead of time. The office was located just down the hallway from the courtroom.

The county attorney's office was located next door, so I stopped in to have a cup of coffee and go over details of the case with Brian and his assistants. I had a great working relationship with all of them. Brian was about the nicest guy I'd ever met, and he had always been willing to listen to any advice or input that I had in a case. In return, I'd always given the same respect to him and his staff. Brian and I are the same age, which makes it easier to relate to each other.

I learned long ago, in my career, it was vitally important to have a close working relationship with their office. Anytime they had a problem in a case and got ahold of me for help, I dropped everything I was doing to solve their problem as soon as possible. Most of the time, the issues were about clarifying something that was not clear to them, such as a lack of evidence in a case, or a request to investigate further, or to locate evidence that had already been obtained, or to obtain further witness and suspect statements.

A lot of times, I heard officers bitching and complaining about the county attorney's office. Usually, this was because the county attorney was asking them to do something further for their case, or the county attorney had to drop the charges in their case due to a lack of evidence, or the evidence being obtained improperly. Sometimes, they had to take a plea agreement to a much lesser charge to get a conviction because the officer's case for the larger charge was weak. I see those instances as the officer's fault, not the county attorney's fault. But that urge to shirk responsibility and blame others speaks volumes to a person's character.

Some officers think once the case is turned over to the county attorney, their job is done unless they get called to testify. It's a foolish officer who thinks that way. A wise officer will keep a close eye on their cases and watch to make sure the criminal charges are filed properly. If the charge was greater or lesser than expected, a diligent officer goes and talks with the county attorney. Most of the time, the disparity can be easily explained and fixed.

A wise officer will always keep their options open. If something new develops in the case after it's been charged, they won't dismiss it. They'll follow up. You can never have too much evidence in a case. A case is never over until the suspect is found guilty or not guilty.

I told Brian and his assistants that if they had any questions or problems with my reports or work in this case, to call me right away so I could fix it. I can't fix something if I don't know it's broken.

Brian told me he would have the criminal complaint drafted by the following day, and Byron would be seen in court sometime that morning. I thanked him for the coffee and all the hard work they did. It never hurts to share a compliment. I then left the office.

My workday was finally coming to an end, but I still had so much to do. I called Chrissy's parents to see if Hailey could spend the next couple of days at their house to help take a little stress off me. Thankfully, they agreed.

At 3:10 p.m. I went to Hailey's school and picked her up. I asked her how her day went, and she told me she'd been tired all day.

"I'm tired too. I'm going to take you over to Grandma and Grandpa for a couple days. Is that okay?"

"Yeah, I like going over there!" I was glad to hear her say that. I then drove her over to Chrissy's parents' house and dropped her off. I still had an hour and a half of my workday left, then I was going to run home, change clothes, and drive to the St. Cloud Hospital to be with Chrissy.

When 5:00 p.m. rolled around, I pulled into my driveway and parked my squad car. I signed off work, then went into the house. I was tired from another long day. As I stood in the bedroom taking off my equipment and uniform, I glanced over at the bed. All I wanted to do was crawl into those blankets, close my eyes, and fall asleep. It was very tempting, but I knew if I did that, I wouldn't make it to the hospital to see my wife. I was already in the doghouse, and I didn't want to tempt fate.

I was changed, out the door, and on the road to St. Cloud by 5:15 p.m. I tuned into my favorite Christmas music station, *Cool 108*. They play continuous Christmas music until after the holidays. I sang along to one of my favorite songs, "Chestnuts Roasting On An Open Fire," and

arrived at the hospital by 5:45 p.m. I stopped by the gift shop and got her some flowers and a balloon. I walked into Chrissy's room and set the flowers and balloon on a stand next to her bed.

Chrissy looked at me. "Thank you, honey, those are beautiful." It felt good to be able to cheer her up. "You look tired. Another long day?"

"Yes, but I'm fine. Just glad to be here with you." The truth was, I wasn't fine. I was exhausted and stressed out, but I wasn't going to tell her that.

As a cop, I'd learned not to show weakness that criminals could try to take advantage of. But this conditioning led me to become very closed off. I tended to bury my emotions. That's frustrating for any spouse.

Chrissy was good at telling me things that bothered her at work, home, or in life in general. Because I love helping people and fixing things, I never minded listening. She told me all the time how frustrated she was with me because I wouldn't tell her what was bothering me, nor did I ever talk about my workday with her.

I guess the reason I didn't talk about stuff is because most of the things I dealt with in my job were bad or sad, and once I got home, I just wanted to forget them. The last thing I wanted to do was talk about the dark stuff when I was at home with my family.

I tended to talk with my fellow officers about my workday problems because we had gone through similar experiences. We leaned on each other for help because we knew the other person would understand what we were going through; they had gone through it too.

I sat in a chair next to her bed as we talked and watched TV together. Chrissy told me to crawl in bed next to her and try to take a little nap. I wanted to do it in the worst way, but I just couldn't bring myself to. I was worried that when the nurse came into the room and saw me lying in bed with her, I would be in their way. I also didn't want them thinking we were doing something we shouldn't be doing in a hospital bed.

I have no doubt that some couples probably do have sex in a hospital room. Looking at all the different positions you can put the bed in, I don't blame them!

But as a cop, I always tried to hold myself and my family to a higher standard because I felt we were in the public's eye, and people loved to spread gossip and rumors.

Time went by fast, and the next thing I knew, it was 8:00 p.m., time for visitors to leave. "I'll be back tomorrow as soon as I can. Love you!" I said.

"Try and get some sleep tonight. I love you too!"

I gave her a kiss, then left the hospital. I got home at 8:30 p.m. and made myself supper since I hadn't eaten yet. I was tired, so I scrounged for something easy to make. I sliced and fried some Spam, toasted bread, and found mustard to make myself a warm Spam sandwich. What is it about Spam that tastes so good? I love the stuff! You're probably thinking because I'm a cop, it must be the pork, right?

I'll never forget one time when I arrested a man for DUI. After I handcuffed him, he kept calling me po-po. I asked him what it meant but he wouldn't tell me. He kept calling me po-po all the way to the jail. When I got him to the jail and was turning him over to the correctional officers, I asked them if they knew what it meant. One of them laughed and said, "It means pig." I wasn't offended, and actually thought it was pretty funny.

I finished my supper, watched a little TV, then went to bed. Again, the bed felt empty and lonely.

Tuesday, November 27, 2012. I woke up at 5:45 a.m., fifteen minutes before the alarm. I crawled out of bed and performed my usual morning routine before work. I was ready and out the door by 6:30 a.m. I got into my squad car and radioed to dispatch that I was in service.

I was in no hurry to get to the office that morning, so I decided to drive to McDonald's and join the coffee clutch. My coffee clutch consisted mostly of my family members, such as my brother, uncles, and cousins. It also consisted of older members of the community.

Of course, the topic of conversation that morning was Byron Smith. I was bombarded with questions about what I knew regarding the case. I hate getting asked these questions because it puts me in a very awkward situation. I can't say much.

"Look, guys. Yes, I was the arresting officer in the case, but that's all I can tell you. I can't talk about the case with anyone." Of course, some of them still tried to ask, fishing for information. All they would get was the same repeated answer. "Sorry, can't talk about it!"

I don't blame them for trying. If I was in their shoes, I would want to know too. If they only knew how lucky they were to not know what I knew. Life would be so much easier. Sometimes, ignorance truly is bliss.

After a half hour of enjoying their company, it was time for me to get to work. I drove around for a little while, patrolling the area and enjoying the Christmas lights that houses and businesses had put up.

When I got to the sheriff's office, I walked into my office and turned on my Christmas lights. I have a string of lights on the front of my desk and a little Christmas tree sitting on the windowsill. My brother Jamie and I are the only deputies that put Christmas lights on our desks in the office.

I'll tell you more about my brother, Deputy Jamie Luberts, in a little while.

As I sat at my desk working on the case, I was thinking about how Byron's first court appearance would go.

In Minnesota, the law states that a person who is arrested must be brought before a judge in the county where the alleged offense occurred, and that this must be done within thirty-six hours of the arrest.

The purpose of the first appearance is for the court to inform the defendant of his or her charges. The court must ensure the person has a copy of the criminal complaint. "These are the criminal charges against the person." Additionally, during this process, the court must set bail and establish other conditions of release. If the court believes the person causes a danger to anyone, he or she could be held in jail. If the person is released, other conditions could be imposed, such as restrictions on travel, or the defendant could be placed under supervision.

By 10:30 a.m., the county attorney's office had drafted the criminal complaint against Byron Smith. The complaint is then sent down to the sheriff's office for review. The complaint must be signed and approved by a deputy and then sent back to the county attorney's office to be sent over to court administrations for the court hearing. In-custodies are typically seen in court around 11:00 a.m.

I reviewed the criminal complaint to make sure it was accurate and the charges were appropriate. There is always a summary written about probable cause in a case with criminal charges. The summary is brief, born of information from the investigative report that I sent to the county attorney. The information outlined in the criminal complaint appeared to be an accurate account of what I had observed and obtained. The charges appeared to be appropriate too. Byron was being charged with two counts of second-degree murder. The criminal complaint was signed and sent back to the county attorney's office.

At 11:00 a.m. I walked upstairs into the courtroom to watch the hearing. It was an open hearing, so anyone could attend. The courtroom was full of people from the public and news media. No cameras were allowed in the courtroom, so all the news reporters had their notepad and pen in their hands, ready to document whatever they could.

There were two separate courtrooms and a stairwell with two holding cells between them. Inmates were brought downstairs from the jail and placed in a holding cell until they were called into court.

When Byron was called into court, he was walked into the courtroom by the bailiff. Our bailiff is one of the department's full-time deputies. Byron was brought over to a table and asked to have a seat next to his defense attorney.

When Byron walked into the courtroom, he was wearing the bright orange clothes of an inmate. His hands were cuffed in front of him, and he had leg shackles securing his ankles. These precautions are meant to prevent anyone in custody from trying to escape.

Back when I first started as a deputy years ago, we didn't put inmates in handcuffs and leg shackles. There were a few times when inmates took advantage of the momentary freedom. Some took off running out of the courtroom. Others would get upset and go after the judge. I was glad when they made it a policy to put all inmates in handcuffs and leg shackles when brought into the courtroom. It was for their safety as well as others'.

The only time inmates are not in jail clothes and handcuffs is during their jury trial or trial in front of a judge.

The judge assigned to the case was the Honorable Douglas Anderson. Judge Anderson asked Byron if he had a chance to review the criminal complaint and the charges against him. Byron said he did. Byron was then explained his legal rights.

Morrison County Attorney Brian Middendorf and his assistant Todd Kosovich were the prosecuting attorneys for the hearing and Steven Meshbesher was the defense attorney for Byron Smith. Both the prosecution and the defense get an opportunity to argue whether there should be bail and how much it should be set at, or whether Byron should be released on his own recognizance pending his next court hearing.

After Judge Anderson listened to both sides, he issued his ruling. Bail was set at one-million-dollar bond or $100,000 cash. I was relieved to hear Judge Anderson set a high bail in this case, not only for Nicholas's and Haile's family's sake, but also for my family's sake. I didn't want my wife to worry about Byron coming after us because he was mad at me for arresting him or for his being charged with two murders.

While I was in court watching Byron's hearing, Little Falls Police Officer Charles Strack, a member of the drug task force, along with deputies from our department and a few BCA agents, executed a search warrant on the southwest side of town.

The BCA had analyzed cellular phones that were recovered from Nicholas and Haile at the crime scene. There were text messages on their phones that indicated juvenile friends of theirs might have been involved in the burglary at Byron's residence and might have been in possession of property stolen from Byron's house. One of the juveniles lived at the address for which we'd obtained the search warrant. I cannot mention the juveniles' names because they are not adults. Juvenile names are kept confidential during any criminal investigation.

Officer Strack had also received information within the past fourteen days that residents at the house in question were suspected of selling and consuming methamphetamine. Thirty-eight-year-old Matthew Kasper rented the house and had a seventeen-year-old son who'd been seen at the residence and was a suspect in burglaries within the surrounding area.

Officers made contact with Matthew Kasper and his seventeen-year-old son at the residence. Officers found drug paraphernalia consisting of a drug scale, baggies, spoons, and syringes. The baggies, spoons, and syringes had residue on them that tested positive for methamphetamine.

Matthew and his seventeen-year-old son were transported to the sheriff's office and both were interviewed regarding the prior burglaries at Byron Smith's residence. Matthew denied knowing where any of the stolen items were. His seventeen-year-old son, however, admitted that the camera that was stolen from Byron's house had once been present at their residence, but he no longer knew where it had gone.

CHAPTER
15

IDENTICAL TWIN DEPUTIES

As you might have noticed, in the first statement I took from Byron, he mentions a deputy by the name of Jamie. That person is Deputy Jamie Luberts. Jamie is my identical twin brother. Jamie and I always had a strong interest in helping people and knew that becoming cops was our shared calling in life.

Police work also runs in our family. Our uncle, Jerry Susalski, was sheriff of Morrison County back when we were kids. He served one term as sheriff and was an investigator and a road deputy for years prior to that. I guess you could say policing is in our blood.

To give you an idea of how identical we are, when we were growing up, our cousins, aunts, uncles, grandparents, and even parents couldn't tell us apart most of the time. We looked alike, walked alike, talked alike, and wore the same matching clothes most of the time. Matching clothes wasn't our idea. Our parents and relatives thought it was cute to dress us alike, so they always bought us the same matching outfits.

At times, Jamie and I had fun confusing people. Other times, I would get blamed for something Jamie did.

Jamie and I graduated high school in the spring of 1992, and in the fall, we started the two-year law enforcement program at Range Technical College located in Hibbing, Minnesota. We were eighteen years old at the time. The program was very strict and intense. It was hard to get into. There was an interview process and a criminal background check conducted prior to being accepted. If you had anything criminal on your record, they wouldn't accept you. Minnesota has a very high standard for its law enforcement officers.

When we started, there were 350 students in the program. When we graduated two years later in the spring of 1994, only fifty of us remained. Most of the students dropped out because they couldn't handle the intensity of the program. Others got kicked out, usually for incurring a criminal charge on their records. Our instructors were all retired law enforcement officers. They told us it was not uncommon for them to see so many people drop out or get kicked out of the program. Not everyone has what it takes to be a cop.

In the summer of 1994, Jamie and I got hired as correctional officers for the Morrison County Sheriff's Office. I'll never forget the words out of our training officers' mouth the first time he saw us. He announced, "We have clones working here!"

In the summer of 1995, I received my license from the State of Minnesota as a law enforcement officer and was appointed by the Morrison County Sheriff, then Paul Tschida, as a patrol officer.

Jamie decided he wanted to go into the military because both of our grandpas had been in the military. He tried talking me into going with him, but I had just started as a patrol officer and wasn't about to give that up for four years.

Jamie and I had been inseparable our whole lives up to that point. Growing up, we got asked all the time if we could read each other's thoughts and feel each other's pain. To both questions, I would have to answer *yes*. There were times when I could feel Jamie's physical and emotional pain.

One time, I asked Jamie to close his eyes and picture a number in his mind between one and ten. I told him I was going to try to read his mind. I closed my eyes and focused with my mind to try to see the number he was thinking of. I was able to see the number he was thinking of every time.

Jamie joined the Navy for four years while I stayed back and worked as a patrol officer. He was stationed in Pearl Harbor, Hawaii. When he was gone for those four years, I felt like I lost half of myself.

Many times, while I was sitting at home alone, I would get a strong sense of feeling homesick. One time, I even felt sick to my stomach for three days and couldn't explain why.

Jamie would call me from time to time and tell me how he missed being home. About a week after feeling sick to my stomach, Jamie called me and said his ship had been sent out to sea about a week ago and went through a typhoon. He told me he got seasick for three days and couldn't eat anything.

When he got out of the Navy, he came back home and got a job as a patrol officer working at the same sheriff's office I did. Being together and working side by side made me feel whole again. We are the first full-time, identical-twin deputy sheriffs to work together in our department. Jamie was hired by our current sheriff, Michel Wetzel.

The University of Minnesota has a twin study they have been doing for many years. Jamie and I have been involved in the twin study. One time, in our mid-twenties, they asked us to come to the university because they had a specific study they wanted to do. It sounded pretty interesting, so we drove down to the university, not knowing what to expect, but thinking we could learn a lot from the experience.

They separated us into different rooms, each with a chair and a TV. A lab student came into the room holding what looked like a shower cap with electrical wires connected to sensors scattered all over the top. He squirted a bunch of jelly inside the cap and said, "I'm going to put this on your head now. Sorry, but this is going to make a mess of your hair." He placed the cap on, and it felt like a lubricated condom had just been put on my head.

The lights were turned off in the room, and I was told to watch the TV monitor. At first, it showed pictures of forests, oceans, various places, animals, and people. Then, all of a sudden, there'd be a picture of a bad accident, a scene where people were badly hurt or even dead. I've been to many bad accident scenes, and have seen people badly hurt. When I was a patrol officer, I saw people who had died in these accidents. Those things no longer fazed me. The images returned to nice scenes again, and then out of the blue, there'd be a picture of a naked lady. Now that caught my attention. This went on for about an hour.

When the test was done, they took the cap off my head and gave me a towel so I could wipe off the gel. I was glad I brought a baseball hat with me. Then the lab student brought me into a different room and conducted an interview with me. He mostly asked questions about my childhood and growing up. That lasted for about another hour, and then I was done with the study.

I waited for Jamie to get done, and we left the university. During the ride back home, we talked about the experience and we both concluded that it was rather weird. We laughed about the pictures of naked girls that would suddenly show up on the screen. We're both pretty sure our brain activity probably spiked off the charts during those pictures. A year later we got the results back from the university. Our brain activity showed that Jamie and I have strikingly similar brain wave patterns that can result in a heightened sense of each other.

I bought a house in Little Falls, and a couple of years after moving there, Jamie bought the house next door. Jamie and I enjoyed living next door to each other, but our wives didn't exactly like it. I don't understand why.

It is confusing as hell for the public, having identical twin deputies working in the same community. Lots of people call into our dispatch center asking to talk with Deputy Luberts. The dispatcher would ask, "Which Deputy Luberts?" The person on the other line would then describe what Deputy Luberts looked like. The dispatcher would have to say, "That doesn't help me. They both look the same."

It would get frustrating for Jamie and me too. When I went to work, the first thing I did each day was check my voicemail, and usually half the messages I got were from people looking to talk with Jamie. Jamie would get the same thing in his voicemail.

One time, I had to testify in court on a speeding ticket I issued to a woman who lived near Little Falls. When it was her turn to testify on the stand, she told the judge the first time I pulled her over, prior to getting this speeding ticket, I was very rude to her.

I told the county attorney, "I've never seen this person before. The only time I met her was this time. When I gave her the speeding ticket, she got all upset with me and started yelling at me. She was very rude to me."

The judge found her guilty, and she had to pay a fine. As we walked out of the courtroom and into the hallway, I asked the lady if I could talk to her. She agreed to talk with me. I told her, "I've never seen you before until just this one time when I had pulled you over."

She told me, "No, you pulled me over before and were very rude to me." I asked her, "Are you aware that I have an identical twin brother who also works as a deputy sheriff in the county?"

She had the "holy shit" look on her face and said, "I had no idea. You have got to be shitting me!" I laughed and said, "Sorry for the confusion, but I do."

Jamie was working that day, and when I met up with him in the office I told him, "Hey, thanks a lot. I just got my ass chewed in court by a lady who thought I was you!"

I told him the lady's name. He started laughing and said, "Yep, that was me. I remember she was kind of rude, so I was rude back to her."

On January 1, 2010, I was promoted to Sergeant Investigator. This title means I'm one of the supervisors among all the deputies, including my brother. It may seem odd that a department would allow that, but everyone knows how well we work together. Plus, if it ever came down to anything involving disciplinary action involving my brother, a different sergeant would handle it. That way, there would not be a conflict of interest.

It's amazing having a twin brother to work with as a deputy sheriff. We have gone through the same things in our jobs, so we both draw strength from each other to deal with the rigors of being a cop. Working with my identical twin is like being able to reach out and connect with myself for help, strength, and advice. Because of our identical genes and very close bond, we're often like two minds working as one.

CONTINUING THE INVESTIGATION

After Byron's court hearing, I went back to my office and did a records search on my computer to see how many burglary or theft complaints Byron reported to our office. To my surprise, I only found one burglary complaint on file. That seemed odd because Byron had told me he reported more than that.

The one and only report I found was a burglary he reported at his residence on 10-27-2012. Jamie was the deputy that responded to the call. Jamie's report said Byron told him he left his house at 11:00 a.m. and when he got home at 6:30 p.m., he found that he'd been broken into.

Byron showed Jamie where someone broke into the downstairs entrance door. Jamie looked at the door and said it looked like someone kicked a hole in the wooden door and then unlocked the dead bolt. He took photographs of the damage.

Jamie said it looked like the suspect had gone through the entire house looking for stuff. He dusted different places in the house that the suspect might have touched, trying to find fingerprints. He was able to find one good fingerprint and he lifted it for evidence by using micro-seal. Micro-seal is an epoxy that comes in two tubes which are similar to toothpaste. One tube is epoxy, and the other is a hardener. First, you squirt out a line of epoxy and then a line of hardener the same length on top of the epoxy. You mix it together with a popsicle stick that comes in the kit and then smear it over the fingerprint that was exposed with the dusting powder. When the epoxy dries, it feels like rubber. That's when you peel the micro-seal off the surface, and you have your suspect's fingerprint.

Once you have a fingerprint on micro-seal, it's virtually indestructible. It's not as clumsy as using clear tape to lift a print. With clear tape, you always run the risk of air bubbles, creases in the tape, and the tape sticking to your rubber gloves. Most of the time you only get one good shot at lifting a fingerprint.

Jamie also obtained a photograph of the suspect's shoe print from the piece of wood that was kicked out of the downstairs entrance door. Jamie asked Byron to stop into our office and have comparison fingerprints done so that we could have them compared to the suspect fingerprint. We do this to make sure the fingerprint found belongs to the suspect, not the homeowner.

Jamie asked Byron if he suspected anyone. Byron told him he thought maybe a couple of his neighbors were to blame. Scott Williams, John Lange, or John's son, Dillan Lange. Byron said he works with kids as a director and is involved with kid activities. He said he would allow Dillan and his friends to rehearse their band in his garage. Byron said it got out of hand when kids started calling a bunch of their friends to show up, so he didn't allow them over anymore. Byron said by allowing this, it made kids aware of where he lived and how secluded his residence is from the road.

I remember Jamie telling me about this burglary back when it happened. I told him to keep following up on the case and let me know if he had any leads.

I found a supplemental report that Jamie dictated on 11-16-2012 regarding a follow-up visit he'd had with Byron at his house. In his report, Jamie said Byron provided him with some paperwork with a value and serial number for the camera that had been stolen in the burglary. The serial number would help us identify Byron's camera if we found it.

Byron showed him locations outside where he had placed surveillance cameras. There's a big tree just off to the right in front of Byron's house. Byron had mounted a camera that would point to the east, and it was hidden under the eve of the house.

He then had Jamie follow him behind the house, where there is an entry door. Byron showed him a wood pile he had stacked to the west of the door, and he had a surveillance camera hidden in the wood pile.

The last place Byron showed him was a surveillance camera that he had mounted on his wooden deck above the rear entry door.

The locations of the surveillance cameras that Byron showed Jamie are the same locations of the surveillance cameras that I found at the house when I arrested Byron.

Byron told Jamie that this was the second time he'd been broken into. He said the first time he didn't report the burglary because he was trying to find out who did it. Byron told him he was going to set up surveillance cameras then, but never got around to it.

Byron told Jamie he had not gone anywhere after this last incident. He said he was sticking around to see if he could catch the people coming back again. Byron told him since this was the second time he was broken into, they would probably attempt to break into his house again. Jamie told Byron if that happened, he needed to call it in right away.

Byron told Jamie that he was also thinking about trying to set up some type of surveillance camera at the end of his driveway. He hadn't done that yet, because there was no electricity down there and he hadn't yet figured out how to do it.

Jamie noted that while speaking with Byron, he seemed very determined to catch the people if they broke into his house again.

I looked at the photograph that Jamie took of the suspect's shoe print on the door panel from the burglary and compared it to the tennis shoes found under the reading chair that belonged to Nicholas Brady. The shoe tread pattern appeared to be a match. That indicated to me that Nicholas probably was responsible for the burglary that Byron reported back in October.

I also found a report written by Deputy Rick Mattison dated 11-21-2012. In his report, he mentioned that a resident who lived off Hilton Road, south of Little Falls, had reported a suspicious vehicle parked halfway down his driveway. He said he didn't know the person in the car. Deputy Mattison and another deputy responded to the location and found Nicholas Brady sitting in the vehicle. When they asked Nicholas why he was parked there, Nicholas told them he wasn't driving the vehicle, but Haile Kifer was. Nicholas said the vehicle had run out of gas and Haile went to look for help. Nicholas was given a ride to Little Falls and Deputy

Mattison patrolled the area, looking for Haile, but was unable to locate her.

The vehicle that Nicholas was in is the 1998 Mitsubishi Eclipse registered to his father, Jason Brady. It's the same vehicle we located about a block away from Byron's house and did a search warrant on.

I did some further digging and found a burglary report dated 11-25-2012. A residence was broken into on Arden Boulevard, south of Little Falls. The residence was only a few blocks away from the address on Hilton Road where contact had been made with Nicholas Brady.

Deputy Dave Scherping was the officer who investigated this burglary. The reporting party told him he was watching the residence for his neighbor who was out of town. He said that his neighbor is a retired schoolteacher. The name of the homeowner is the same name on the prescription pill bottles I found in the vehicle that Nicholas and Haile were driving.

Dave met with the reporting party at the residence and saw the southeast patio door was smashed in. He checked the inside of the residence and noticed in every room in the house, there were open dresser drawers and open boxes. The homeowner hadn't been home since 11-12-2012.

Dave noted that he made phone contact with the homeowner the next day after the homeowner returned home. The homeowner told him, from what he could determine at that time, that he was missing five of his medication bottles; fifty to sixty foreign coins, both copper and silver; and a gold wristwatch. These stolen items appeared to be the same items I found in the Mitsubishi Eclipse.

I called the homeowner and asked him to come into the sheriff's office so I could show him the items I recovered from the car. He said he would stop by in a couple days.

It was getting close to five o'clock. It was another night of getting off work, changing my clothes, then going straight to the hospital to be with my wife.

I made it to the hospital at 5:50 p.m. Chrissy was looking and feeling much better. She told me if her blood test results came back good, she would be allowed to return home the following day. I was really looking forward to that. It would be nice to stay at home with my family for a change.

I was also looking forward to making a home-cooked meal. I do most of the cooking at home. I'm good at it, thanks to my mom. I can't blame Chrissy for not being a good cook, but I do blame her mother.

One time, when we were visiting her parent's house, her mom made chili. Chrissy set a bowl in front of me, and I asked her what it was.

"It's my mom's chili. Try it."

It didn't look like chili, just tomato juice and hamburger. Not wanting to be rude, I tried it. Yuck. I was right; it was just a bowl of tomato juice and hamburger.

Chrissy told me coworkers of hers had been stopping by her room to visit. She said all of them knew that I was an investigator for the sheriff's office and had asked her questions about the case.

"Now I know why you don't talk about your work with me. I told them I don't know what's going on, and that's the truth. I don't know because you never tell me anything."

"That's a good thing. Trust me, it's far better for you not to know."

"Well, it doesn't make it any easier. Some of them told me they're glad Byron is in jail for killing those two teenagers, and others told me it's wrong that he was arrested. They said the teenagers got what they deserved for breaking into his house."

Just great, I thought. Now I'd have to worry about how my family was going to be treated by certain people in the community because I did my job. It's funny how people love to jump to conclusions without knowing the facts.

I told Chrissy the only thing I could tell her. "I'm sorry you have to deal with this too just because you're my wife. I know it's not fair that people are going to be upset with you because of me, but trust me when I tell you I had no choice in the decisions I made. I can't help what others are going to think or say about me."

I could tell Chrissy was worried about the backlash from this case; I could see that it was bothering her a lot.

CHAPTER
17

COMING HOME

Wednesday, November 28, 2012 was my day off, so I slept in until 8:00 a.m. I woke up, made a pot of coffee, turned on my electric fireplace, and sat in the living room. I stared out the window at the black and gray squirrels chasing each other up the trees in the front yard. Everything looked so beautiful covered in snow.

A lot of people complain about the snow and the cold, but I love it. Fall and winter are the perfect temperatures for me. Anything above seventy degrees and I'm sweating.

I set the thermostat in my house at sixty-six degrees during the winter. It took me a while, but I finally got Chrissy and Hailey comfortable with the idea.

When it's cold outside, you can always put on more clothes to keep warm. It's not so easy to get comfortable when it's hot out. Legally, you can only take off so many clothes. It's not like you can run around naked or in your underwear. At least not here in Minnesota.

As I sat drinking my coffee, my thoughts drifted off to a few years back, a summer when I got called in to investigate an older male party that was walking around naked in his yard and on his dock at his lake cabin on Lake Sullivan.

The cabin is located on the northeast end of our county. Our office received multiple calls from multiple people who had seen the naked old man while driving by his dock in their boats. When I pulled into the driveway, I saw the old man outside walking toward the front entry door to the house, and sure enough, he was naked! His gray-haired balls and wrinkled pecker were flopping in the breeze. He saw me pull into his driveway, and his naked old ass scurried into the house. There are some things in life you just can't unsee.

I walked up to the front door and knocked. It took about five minutes for the man to answer the door, and when he did, he was only wearing a towel wrapped around his waist. I told him the sheriff's office had received complaints of him walking around outside naked, and that when I pulled into his driveway, I had seen him walking to the house naked. I asked him to tell me why he was doing that.

The man said, "Well, it's my cabin, and I came up here from the cities to enjoy myself and be one with nature."

I asked the man how old he was, and he said seventy-two.

I told him, "Sir, at seventy-two, you should know better than to be walking around outside naked. There are children outside that don't need to see that. What I should do is arrest you for indecent exposure."

The man said, "No, please officer, don't arrest me. I don't know how I would explain that to my wife. She would be really mad at me."

I went back to my squad car and ran a criminal background check on the man. He had no prior offenses on his record.

"I'm going to give you a verbal warning this time, but if I ever catch you doing this again, the first thing I'm going to do is call your wife, and after that, I'll arrest you and haul you to jail." The man was very grateful for the break and swore he'd never do it again.

I left his residence and called the complainants back to inform them what I did. They were grateful that I talked with the man and had given him a second chance. I told them if they saw him do it again, to call me and next time he would be arrested. They couldn't help but laugh about the situation, and neither could I. I'm pretty sure the old pervert learned his lesson. Our office didn't receive any further calls regarding that matter.

It's memories like those that kept the job fun and interesting. From one day to the next, I never knew what I'd run into.

At 11:00 a.m., I got a call from Chrissy. She told me her blood test results came back normal. She could come home. I told her I'd be there to pick her up in about an hour. I got dressed and headed out the door. I was excited to finally bring Chrissy home.

When I got to the hospital, Chrissy was waiting for me in her room. I gathered her belongings, and out the door we went. When we got back to Little Falls, we stopped at her parents' residence so I could pick up Hailey's stuff while she was at school. After visiting for a little while, we went home.

Chrissy was still feeling weak, so she went into the bedroom and lay down. Hailey's school day was nearly over, so I drove to the school to pick her up.

"Guess what?" I said when we got into my truck. "I have a surprise for you when we get home."

"What is it?"

"You will just have to wait and see."

When I pulled into the driveway, Hailey couldn't get out of the truck fast enough. She ran into the house as I followed a short distance behind. "Mommy, you're home! I missed you so much!"

I couldn't help but think about Nicholas's and Haile's parents. What they wouldn't give to have this kind of home-coming reunion again.

OTHERS INVOLVED

Thursday, November 29, 2012. It was morning, and I was sitting in my office going over details of the Smith case.

Officer Chuck Strack called me and said, "I'm going to apply for another search warrant at Matthew Kasper's residence to look for the stolen camera that Matthew's son admitted in his statement was at his house."

"Let me know when it's ready and I'll meet you at the residence."

A few hours later, Chuck called me and said he got the search warrant approved. Chuck, a couple agents from the BCA, a couple officers from the Little Falls Police Department, one of my fellow deputies, and I responded to the Kasper residence.

When we arrived, Matthew came out to meet us. We told Matthew we had a search warrant for his residence, and we asked him to step back inside his house. We then followed him into the residence.

Inside, Chuck told Matthew, "We know you were not being truthful with us in your knowledge of the stolen property and the burglary at Byron Smith's residence."

Matthew became agitated. "I talked with my son the evening of November 28 regarding the burglary. He told me one of the guns taken in the burglary was given to a friend of his in return for a space heater. He didn't say anything about a camera."

Chuck asked Matthew where his son currently was, and Matthew said, "At school." Chuck then asked Matthew if he would call Little Falls High School and give permission for his son to get out of school so we could do a follow-up interview with him. Matthew agreed and called the school.

Two of the officers at the scene left the residence and drove to the school to meet with Matthew's son while the rest of us searched for the camera. Approximately thirty minutes later, we received a phone call from one of the officers who interviewed Matthew's son. He said Matthew's son told them his dad had the camera and had given it to his friend, Ray Morris.

Chuck again asked Matt about the Nikon camera. Matthew said he never saw the camera, didn't know where it was, and that his son was lying.

We called Ray Morris, who told us Matthew had tried to sell him the camera on the night of November 29, after the first search warrant, and after Matthew knew police were looking for it. We were then informed Matthew had sent a kid to dispose of the camera by throwing it in the Mississippi river.

Chuck was given a location where the camera was dumped. It was just off Lindbergh Drive Southwest, near a boat landing south of Lindbergh State Park. Chuck left the residence and drove to the location to look for the camera while the other officers and I stayed at the residence and continued the search.

When Chuck arrived at the location, he saw a black plastic bag in the water. He fished it out, and inside was the Nikon camera and lens that had been stolen from Byron Smith's residence. Chuck photographed the items and collected them as evidence.

Chuck radioed to us that he recovered the stolen camera. We then told Matthew he was under arrest for obstructing legal process, possession of stolen property, and fifth-degree possession of a controlled substance from the previous search warrant at his residence.

Matthew was handcuffed and escorted to the back seat of a squad car. Matthew was then transported to the Morrison County Jail and booked in on his new charges.

After leaving a copy of the search warrant and an evidence receipt, we secured the front door of his house, then cleared the residence.

I drove back to the sheriff's office to follow up on Matthew's claims that one of his son's friends was in possession of a firearm stolen from Smith's residence.

Back at the office, I met with Agent Museus, who interviewed Kasper's son. He told me the juvenile admitted to taking possession of the stolen Nikon camera and lens from his friend, Nicholas Brady. He also got the name of the friend who was supposedly in possession of a firearm stolen from Smith's residence. Officers were informed that the juvenile who was in possession of the firearm, which was described as a 12-gauge shotgun, came into possession of the gun after trading a space heater for it.

Nicholas was clearly involved in the home burglary Byron reported to my brother back in October, and he was getting rid of the stolen property by trading it to his juvenile friends.

Sheriff Wetzel was given an update on the progress of the investigation. Michel said, "I know the juvenile who is supposed to be in possession of this firearm, and I also know his parents. I'll follow up with him and his parents to try to recover the firearm."

I respected Michel for being willing to drop what he was doing to get his hands dirty in this case. Michel was the type of boss that was intensely serious when need be, but then could lighten the mood with a practical joke when the time was right.

One day, I was on the telephone in my office talking with someone and my ear started to burn. It felt like it was on fire. It didn't take me long to figure out someone had put pepper spray on my handset. I instantly had my suspicions about who the culprit was.

Michel was in his office and I heard him say, "Son of a bitch, there it is!" Chief Deputy Thomas Ploof and I walked into his office and asked him what was up. Michel said, "Some asshole hid what looks like an egg salad sandwich behind a drawer in my desk. I've been trying to find this rotten smell in my office for the past month and I finally found it!" Tom and I almost pissed our pants from laughing so hard.

Dispatch radioed me and said the schoolteacher who reported a burglary at his residence in November was at the front desk asking to meet with me. This schoolteacher was the same person whose name was on the prescription pill bottles that I found in Nicholas Brady's vehicle.

I went to my evidence locker and grabbed the items I recovered from the vehicle and set them on my desk. I then went to the lobby to greet the schoolteacher. I thanked him for coming in and asked him to walk with me back to my office. There, I showed him the items.

He identified the collectible coins and bills, some of the jewelry, and the prescription pill bottles as the property stolen from his house. The last item of evidence I showed him was the black Calvin Klein bag. From his first glance at the bag, I noticed he had a rather peculiar look on his face. I unzipped the bag and showed him the contents inside.

I must admit, I was having fun with this. I knew this item was going to make him squirm. I couldn't stop myself from asking, "I think this is a dildo and anal beads. Are these yours also?" The look on his face said it all.

"I'm embarrassed to say, but those are mine as well."

I fought very hard to keep a straight face. I looked at him and said, "I don't judge people. What you do in private is your own business. Unfortunately, it's my job to confirm these things. Thank you for your help in this matter."

He looked at me and said, "Thank you for understanding."

I told him I had to keep the items as evidence for now, but that he would get them back when the case was over. I thanked him for his assistance and then walked him back to the lobby.

After he left, I put the items of evidence back in my evidence locker for safekeeping.

Michel drove to the residence of the juvenile who was suspected of being in possession of the stolen shotgun. The kid was in his teens, and lived south of Little Falls. Michel met him in his driveway. He asked him to have a seat in the front of his squad car. The juvenile agreed and Michel told him why he was there. He asked the boy if he was in possession of a shotgun he'd received from a friend.

The juvenile told him he was, and immediately insisted that until the day prior, he'd had no idea the weapon was stolen. He went on to tell him he traded his Friction bicycle for the 12-gauge shotgun. His juvenile friend was supposed to pay an additional twenty dollars as part of the bargain but never did.

The juvenile told Michel the exchange occurred a month and half ago, and that he'd retained possession of the shotgun until yesterday, when his friend Kasper approached him in school and told him the shotgun had been stolen from the Smith residence, and he should get rid of it. The juvenile said he was quite scared after learning that, and so he took the gun to a swampy area on Joe Doty's property and hid it.

The juvenile told Michel he intended to speak with his mother to try to find a way to return the gun or turn it over to authorities without getting in trouble. He said he was upset his friend would have traded him a stolen gun, and he'd talked to his friend about it. He asked his friend what he thought they should do. His friend told him, "Don't tell anything to the cops about it, and I won't either."

The juvenile agreed to show Michel where the gun was. He directed Michel to a location on 140 Avenue in Belleview Township on the north side of a wooded trail. From there, they walked directly into a swamp, and the boy pointed into the grass where the shotgun lay. There was snow on the weapon, but no rust. The gun did not appear to have been lying there long.

Michel took photographs of the shotgun, then retrieved it from its spot in the grass and placed it in his squad car for evidence. The Remington 12-gauge shotgun matched the description of the shotgun stolen from Smith's residence.

When Michel got back to the office, he placed the shotgun in an evidence locker to secure it. Michel then made phone contact with Smith's attorney, Steven Meshbesher. Michel told Steven he wanted to speak to Byron only for the purpose of allowing Byron to positively identify the recovered weapon. Michel sent his request to Meshbesher in writing. A short time later, he received a fax from Meshbesher's office stating he was not authorized to speak to his client at all about the incident.

It's stuff like that that makes the job so frustrating. We knew for sure it was Smith's shotgun. We just wanted confirmation from him. The confirmation helps us to charge the juveniles who were in possession of the stolen property.

Morrison County Sheriff's Deputy Jason McDonald, who works on the drug task force, was asked to try to contact the juvenile that traded the shotgun to the friend who was caught with it.

Jason drove to the juvenile's residence located off 6th Street Southwest in Little Falls. The juvenile's mother, Danielle Kriesel, answered the door. Jason told Danielle he was looking for her son. Her son came to the door and was initially upset that Jason was there. Danielle refused to let her son go with Jason. Jason explained to Danielle that he believed her son was involved in a burglary and wanted to talk with him and ask him questions at the sheriff's office. Danielle agreed to let her son be brought into the sheriff's office for questioning. She was also fine with him not having a lawyer present during his questioning.

Jason had Kriesel's son accompany him to his squad car and have a seat inside. Jason then cleared the residence and brought the juvenile to the sheriff's office.

Some people think it's against the law for cops to talk with a juvenile without the parents' consent or presence at the interview. That's not true. We don't need parental consent, and we never allow anyone besides cops, social workers, and attorneys to be present in the interview room when we are taking statements from a suspect, no matter their age.

It's our department's policy to try to notify parents before questioning any juvenile. We also ask for consent from the parents to talk with their child without a lawyer present. If the parent says *no* and wants a lawyer for their child, we will not attempt a statement without a lawyer present. The only time we don't notify a parent is if they are a suspect in the case.

When Jason got back to the office, he brought Kriesel into the interview room and activated his digital recorder. He then read Kriesel his Miranda warning legal rights. Kriesel said he understood his rights and agreed to talk with Jason.

During Kriesel's interview, he denied any involvement in the burglary at Byron Smith's residence but did admit to having possession of a 12-gauge shotgun. He said he got the shotgun from Nick Brady, who had stolen it from Smith's residence. Kriesel admitted that he traded the shotgun to a friend of his earlier this fall in exchange for a bike and an electric heater.

Jason then asked Kriesel about his involvement with Nick. Kriesel said he was very good friends with Nick and had hung out with him several days a week throughout the summer. Kriesel said he was at the Brady residence in the Enchanted Lakes area on several occasions.

Eventually, during questioning, Kriesel admitted he had been at the Byron Smith residence with Nick earlier that year, but he said he had not entered the residence. They left because someone was home.

Kriesel also said Nick had stolen a large sum of cash and some war medals from Smith. Kriesel continued to deny being involved in any burglaries with Nick, but did say he had seen several items that he believed were stolen throughout his time of hanging out with Nick.

When Jason concluded his statement with Kriesel, he took him home and explained to Danielle what her son had been involved in. Kriesel was then left in the custody of his mother for the time being.

ANOTHER SEARCH WARRANT AT SMITH'S RESIDENCE

I walked into the county attorney's office to meet with Brian and fill him in on what we'd recently discovered. I told Brian the reports regarding criminal charges against Kasper and Kriesel would be submitted to his office in a couple of days. Their charges would be for their part in the possession of stolen property from Smith's residence.

"It's clear to us now that Nick and Haile were involved in the burglary of Smith's residence back in October. They went back to Smith's to try again, not knowing that this time, he'd set a trap for them. The trap wasn't illegal until Smith decided to take revenge rather than seek justice in this matter."

"I agree. I'm glad you guys were able to solve the burglary of Smith's residence. I will definitely file charges against the other people involved. Now I need you to do something else."

"Anything you need. What's up?"

"I called the Minnesota State Attorney General's Office to ask for their help in the murder charges against Smith.

They have more experience in prosecuting murder cases than we do, and I was hoping their attorneys would take the lead in this case. They also have more time to invest in this than we do. We have a lot of other court hearings and trials pending. They haven't given me an answer yet as to whether they will take the case, but they did suggest that we do another search warrant at Smith's residence."

That surprised me. "What for? I thought we got everything we needed from the house."

"They think it's a good idea to go back and look for any electronics such as cell phones and computers, *especially* computers, and have the BCA analyze them to see if Byron talked about or searched for information regarding a plan to set a trap or kill someone."

"That's a good idea. I had so much to do, that I didn't even think about that," I admitted. "I'll get on it right away."

I left Brian's office and went back to the sheriff's office. I met with the BCA agents in our conference room and told them about Brian's request. They all agreed it was a good idea, something they, too, had overlooked seizing when we did the initial search warrant.

It's always good to have as many eyes on a case as possible so something like this doesn't get missed.

Agent Museus and I met in my office and drafted another search warrant for Smith's residence to look for electronic items. I've drafted many search warrants in my career, so it didn't take me long to complete this one.

When the search warrant was ready, I walked upstairs to the court administration's office and met with the Honorable Conrad Freeberg to have it signed and approved.

I've gotten to know Judge Freeberg pretty well. He was the Morrison County Attorney for many years before he became a judge. Freeberg prosecuted many of my cases I investigated. We had gained a mutual respect throughout the years.

After the warrant was approved, I walked back downstairs and met with the BCA agents to make plans to go back to Smith's residence. When we left Smith's residence after completing the first search warrant, we locked and secured all the doors. We knew Byron's brother Bruce was currently staying at the house because he told officers he would be taking care of the place for a little while.

The BCA agents and I left the sheriff's office and drove to Smith's residence. We arrived at the residence at 3:49 p.m. and didn't see any vehicles parked in the yard. I knocked on the front door and announced, "Sheriff's office, search warrant." There was no answer at the door, and I couldn't see any lights on in the house. Bruce didn't appear to be around. I checked the door, and it was locked.

With the search warrant in hand, I had the right to force my way into the residence, but I don't like damaging anyone's property if I don't have to.

I remember one time when I was executing a search warrant on an old, run-down trailer house. The front entry door was wood, and I had to force entry to get inside. I gave the door a mighty kick and when I did, I expected the door to fly open, but it didn't. Instead, my foot went through the door. They had a good deadbolt lock, but the door was a piece of shit. It's usually the other way around. The door is good, and the lock is bad. It turned out nobody was home, and later, I had to explain to the owner of the property why there was a hole in his front door.

We had a cell phone number listed in our records for Bruce, so I tried calling him. I was able to reach him, and he said he was currently at a business in Little Falls. Bruce agreed to come back to the residence and meet with us. He arrived shortly, and I presented the search warrant to him.

"Has anybody else been inside the residence besides you?" I asked Bruce.

"No, it's just been me."

"Have you removed anything from inside the residence?"

"No, I haven't."

Bruce agreed to unlock the door so we could conduct our search. Bruce stayed in the house the entire time, watching us, as we searched his brother's home. Inside, BCA agents seized multiple electronic devices, including a laptop computer, computer tower, multiple memory discs, SD cards, and thumb drives. Every item was logged onto an evidence receipt.

When we completed our search, I left a copy of the search warrant and evidence receipt on the kitchen table. I thanked Bruce for his cooperation, and we then cleared from the residence.

The BCA agents kept the evidence to bring back to their lab. I don't envy the BCA lab technician who had to process that evidence. It was certain to be a very long and tedious process.

A GOOD IDEA

On the morning of Friday, November 30, 2012, Sheriff Wetzel and I were talking in his office, having our cups of coffee, and wondering how we could get the recovered shotgun identified. After pondering on it for a little while, I finally had an idea.

"Byron told me he got the shotgun from his father. I'm guessing his brother Bruce probably saw the shotgun when his dad used it."

"That's a good idea. Call Bruce and see if he will come into the office to meet with us."

Bruce answered his phone right away and agreed to come into the office that afternoon.

Bruce arrived at the sheriff's office at 2:50 p.m. Michel and I met with him in our interview room. Michel told Bruce, "We've been working on the burglary case Byron reported, and I recovered a Remington 12-gauge shotgun."

"My father use to own a gun like that and gave it to Byron." Michel then showed the shotgun to Bruce. Bruce studied the gun. "This gun was my father's, and now Byron owns it. I held this gun many times in the past. I can tell it's his by the engraved picture of a duck in the metal, the wear on the gun, and the crack in the wooden stock."

"Well, I'm glad we could recover some of your brother's stolen property," Michel said.

"We'll have to hold onto the gun as evidence for now. We have two suspects who will be charged for possession of stolen property regarding Byron's burglary at his residence. When the cases are over, we can release the property back to you," I explained.

We thanked Bruce for coming into the office and identifying the gun for us. I then walked him back to the lobby, and he left. I placed the shotgun back into our evidence locker for safekeeping.

I went back into my office to dictate a supplemental report regarding the incident. As I was talking into my digital recorder, Jamie dropped by.

"How are things going?"

"Pretty good. We were able to recover the Nikon camera and Remington 12-gauge shotgun that were stolen during Smith's burglary. We have two suspects that will be charged."

"Good. I was hoping we would figure something out in this burglary case. You need me to do anything?"

"No. Just make sure you have all your paperwork and reports done. I'm going to send everything up to the county attorney for charges as soon as I get my report done."

"I have everything done and ready to go." Jamie then asked, "How's everything going at home?"

"Not so good. Chrissy's feeling better, but she's afraid Byron is going to get out of jail and come after us because I arrested him. She's also worried about how people will treat her when she goes back to work because of my involvement in this case."

"Yeah, that sucks. It's not like it's our fault that Byron's sitting in jail charged with two murders. We just did our jobs."

"I know. But try telling that to the people who think Byron had the right to protect himself in his own home. It's all over the news that he shot and killed two intruders that broke into his home. The problem is, they don't know the rest of the story. Keep an eye out when you're at home for anything suspicious happening in our neighborhood. Also, be careful when you're out in public. Don't talk about the case, and be on guard for people who might be upset with us."

"I'll tell Jennifer to keep a close lookout at home. We can try and keep an eye out for each other."

I then held out my fist in front of him and said, "Wonder twin powers." Jamie touched his fist with mine. "Activate."

Jamie and I loved watching *Super Friends* when we were kids. The wonder twins were our favorite and would do this to activate their powers. We've done this at work in front of coworkers too. They roll their eyes at us and tell us we're weird.

Jamie and I just tell them they're jealous because they don't have a wonder twin.

AMAZING DISCOVERY

A week went by, and I was busy in my office working on new cases. As I was looking at information on my computer, Michel came in.

"I just got off the phone with the BCA, and you'll never guess what they found."

"Please," I said looking up at him, "tell me it's good news."

"Agent Janet Nelson was working on the two digital recorders found in Byron's house. The recorder that was in the bookshelf above his reading chair recorded the whole incident."

I thought to myself, *Oh, you mean the one with the dead batteries that the BCA wanted nothing to do with. The one I demanded they take and analyze.* But I wouldn't say that out loud. I'm not about being a smartass, but it was validating to know my instincts had been right.

I had learned through years of experience that it's always a good policy to take a final look around before completing a search warrant. This is especially true if multiple officers were involved. Often, I or other officers would find something that had been overlooked during the initial search.

Michel asked me if I wanted to listen to the recording.

"Um . . . let me think. Yes, I want to listen to it!"

Michel and I then went into his office and listened to the recording. The initial recording is six hours and twenty-four minutes long. Agent Nelson condensed the recording down to the important evidentiary parts because there are a lot of footsteps, heavy breathing, and long periods of silence in between. That recording is twenty-nine minutes long. No jury would want to sit through almost six and a half hours when the important information is only twenty-nine minutes long. I was grateful Agent Nelson took her time to do this.

Michel started the recording. I could hear Byron Smith talking, in what sounded like a rehearsed conversation, with his brother, Bruce. "In your left eye . . . Stop by tomorrow morning. No rush, but as soon as it is convenient. Can you do that? Yeah. Uh, park to the north, one hundred feet nor . . . one hundred yards north of the corner and walk from the west."

I also heard Byron say, "I realize I don't have an appointment, but I would like to see one of the lawyers here."

There was a pause, and then I heard what sounded like a window shattering in the distance. A short time later, I heard footsteps walking down a hallway, getting louder and obviously nearer to the recording device. There was a brief pause, and then the sound of two footsteps coming down the stairs. Suddenly, two shots rang out. I heard a moan in a male vocal range and then someone tumbling down the stairs. I heard another shot and then Byron saying, "You're dead."

Next, I could hear the rustling of a tarp, then something being placed on and wrapped in the tarp. I could hear the tarp dragging across the floor, getting further away into a different room. A short time later, I could hear the metal sliding noise of bullets being loaded into a gun in the same room the recorder was in.

Byron was breathing heavily, moving closer to the recorder, and it sounded like he sat back down in a chair.

Eleven minutes passed. Then I heard more footsteps in the hallway upstairs. They were getting louder and closer. There was another brief pause, and then I heard a female voice whisper, "Nick, Nick." She waited briefly. Then I heard her footsteps coming down the stairs. A shot rang out and again I heard someone falling down stairs. Then I heard a click, like a gun had jammed and failed to fire.

I heard Byron say, "Oh, sorry about that." Then I heard the female desperately saying in a pleading voice, "Oh my God . . . I'm sorry!" Multiple more shots followed, and I heard Haile screaming. Byron yelled, "You're dying!" When the shooting was over, I heard Byron's cruel voice. "Bitch."

I heard dragging again, but this time it was clothes on carpet getting distant until, from some ways off, I could hear the rustling of the tarp again. When the rustling stopped, there was a short silence, and then a final, distant shot. All the other shots had sounded close. This final shot was remote and muffled.

Later in the recording, Byron makes dozens of statements. Some are fully audible. Others are difficult to hear. This is what I heard:

"I left my house at 11:30. They were both dead by 1 . . ."

"Cute. I'm sure she thought she was a real pro . . ."

"You're dead . . ."

"I am not a bleeding-heart liberal. I felt like I was cleaning up a mess. Not like spilled food. Not like vomit. Not even like . . . not even like diarrhea. The worst mess possible. And I was stuck with it . . ."

"In some tiny little respect . . . in some tiny little respect . . . I was doing my civic duty. If the law enforcement system couldn't handle it, I had to do it. I had to do it . . ."

"The law system couldn't handle her, and it fell into my lap, and she dropped her problem in my lap . . ."

"And she threw her problem in my face. And I had to clean it up . . ."

"They weren't human. I don't see them as human. I see them as vermin. Social mistakes. Social problems. I don't see them as . . . human. This bitch was going to go through her life, destroying things for other people. Thieving, robbing, drug use . . ."

"It's all fun. Cool. Exciting. Highly profitable. Until somebody kills you . . ."

"It's a sucker shot. People going down strange stairs naturally watch the steps . . ."

"Like I give a damn who she is . . ."

"It's not a mess like spilled food. It's not a mess like vomit. It's not even a mess like diarrhea. It's far worse. Then they take slice after slice out of me . . ."

"Five thousand. Five-thousand-dollar slice. Ten-thousand-dollar slice. And if I gather enough evidence, they might be prosecuted. If they're prosecuted, it might go to court. If it goes to court, they might be found guilty . . ."

"If they're found guilty, they might spend . . . six months, two years in jail, and then they're out, and they need money worse than ever, and they're filled with revenge. I cannot live a life like that . . ."

"I cannot have that chewing on me for the rest of my life. I cannot . . . I refuse to live with that level of fear in my life. I refuse to live with that level of fear in my life . . ."

"She's tough. She's eye candy. It's games. It's exciting. It's highly profitable. Until somebody kills you. Until you go too far, and somebody kills you. Until you take advantage of somebody who's not a sucker . . ."

"Mother and father are semi-psychotic, are both semi-psychotic. I put even odds that one or the other will come over here with a gun . . ."

I just stood there, stunned. I told Michel it was like finding the holy grail of evidence.

"This recording was given to the county attorney."

"I bet he shits himself when he listens to it."

The next day, I went to the county attorney's office and talked with Brian. I asked him what he thought about the recording we found.

"This was a first for me. It's very rare to hear a murder take place and the suspect's state of mind before and after it happens. It was chilling to listen to," he said.

"I almost shit myself when I heard it," I confided.

"Yeah, me too."

Brian told me Smith's attorney was requesting another hearing soon to seek a bail reduction. Brian said they could use this new evidence to argue that Smith's bail should be raised, in the hopes that he could not be bailed out of jail before his trial.

"That would be good for the victim's family as well as mine. My wife is worried that Byron might come after me and my family if he gets released. I told her not to worry, but to tell you the truth, I'm a little worried myself."

A few days later, Agent Nelson told us she was able to retrieve video footage from Smith's home surveillance recording system. Nelson was able to get the twenty-four hours before and after the shootings occurred, from November 21 to the 23.

The four-camera video showed that at approximately 11:30 a.m. on Thanksgiving Day, November 22, 2012, Smith moved his pickup from his garage and drove it away from his residence.

At 11:45 a.m., Smith walked through the woods to his backyard, which faced the river, instead of approaching his home's main entrance from the street.

At 12:33 p.m., Nicholas Brady approached Smith's house, looked into the windows, and tried the doorknobs. At one point, Brady spotted one of the four cameras hidden atop a wood pile near the lower-level back entry door and turned it so that the camera view was obscured.

Another camera view showed Haile Kifer waiting just past the tree line on the north side of Smith's property.

At 12:39 p.m., Nicholas walked across the deck on the upper level of the home. That's the last we see of him on camera.

At 12:50 p.m., Haile approached the residence carrying a large purse. She checked the doors. That's the last we see of her on camera.

There were four cameras, and all of them were outside. There were no cameras in the house.

Agent Nelson said they would make sure this new evidence got to the county attorney's office for review.

BAIL HEARING

On Monday, December 17, 2012, Smith's bail hearing was held in the Morrison County courtroom in front of Judge Douglas Anderson. Smith and his lawyer, Steve Meshbesher, were present. The prosecutors present were Morrison County Attorney Brian Middendorf and his assistant, Todd Kosovich.

I sat in the back of the courtroom and watched the hearing. Multiple news media outlets were present, but no video cameras were allowed in the courtroom. Byron's brother, Bruce Smith, and relatives of Brady and Kifer were also present.

Kosovich told the court, "The state will show that this was an ambush, and a murder."

Kosovich went on to tell the court that Smith was charged with two counts of second-degree murder in the deaths of Brady and Kifer, teenagers who were breaking into Smith's red-brick rambler along the Mississippi River when he shot them and dragged their bodies into a workshop, where they remained for more than twenty-four hours.

Kosovich said that on the day of the killings, Smith had guns within reach as he sat in a chair, between tall bookshelves, facing the basement stairs.

"He had unscrewed light bulbs from sockets. There was a loaded rifle next to him and a loaded .22-caliber revolver strapped to his side. Search warrants have revealed that Smith, a former security engineer for US embassies, also had a surveillance system that picked up images of Kifer and Brady outside his home. Inside the house, police found hours of audiotapes on a digital recorder."

Kosovich said, "A recording includes the sound of breaking glass, presumably when Brady broke a rear window, crawled in, and then went downstairs. Smith shot Brady three times, telling him, 'You're dead,' according to the recording. Just eighteen seconds later, there's the sound of Brady's body being dragged on a tarp to a workshop. That's how fast, that's how well-equipped he was to deal with the death of Nick Brady. Ten minutes after the last shot, as Smith sat in his chair, Kifer's voice can be heard on the tape, calling out 'Nick?' Twelve seconds pass, and Kifer begins down the stairs. Then we hear the first shot, and the sound of her body falling down the stairs. Smith's rifle jams. The click is audible, and Smith is heard saying, 'Oh, sorry about that.'

"As Kifer moans, Smith switches to the revolver. After the second shot, Kifer says, 'Oh, my God,' and on the third shot, 'Oh, God.' After the fourth shot, she utters, 'Aw,' and Smith says to her, 'You're dying.'"

Then Kosovich says, "She's on the basement floor, helpless, and Smith calls her 'bitch.' The sound of Smith dragging her to his workshop is audible and she is heard gasping. One minute and fifteen seconds later, again calling her *bitch*, Smith fired a shot beneath her chin and into her cranium. He shot Haile Kifer three times in the head. There's no way that's self-defense.

"From the sound of the window breaking to when Brady

came downstairs, seven minutes passed during which Smith could have called the police."

Kosovich then quoted Smith's description of Kifer's death to police. "She gave out the death twitch; it works the same as in a beaver or deer."

In the courtroom audience, one of the teen's family members could be heard whispering, "Oh, my God."

In asking for lower bail, Meshbesher said Smith was a Little Falls native who retired after working sixteen years at a computer job with the Department of Homeland Security.

Meshbesher also said Smith had written a memo to the sheriff's office about his October 27 burglary and others in the area. His basement door, on a walkout level, had been kicked in, a lock broken, and guns, cash, and other items stolen.

"He told the police his story because he wanted their assistance and guidance. He was a concerned, good citizen."

Kosovich argued that Smith was a danger to the community, noting that "he admitted he sat with the bodies for twenty-four hours."

A neighbor, William Anderson, contacted the sheriff's office twenty-four hours after the slayings because Smith called him asking if he knew a good attorney.

After hearing the arguments, Judge Anderson made a ruling that reduced Smith's bail from one-million-dollar bond or $100,000 cash to half-a-million-dollar bond or $50,000 cash. Smith had to surrender his passport and guns and not leave the state without the court's consent.

When the hearing was over, Byron was brought back into the jail and the courtroom cleared.

I walked out of the courtroom very disappointed by the judge's decision. I was dumbfounded by how a judge could lower the bail on someone who had just murdered two people.

I hoped Byron wouldn't come up with the bail money. If he got released, I wasn't sure how I'd explain it to Chrissy. I could barely understand the logic of that ruling myself. And she was already a nervous wreck over all this.

That night, friends of Byron and his brother, Bruce, came into the sheriff's office and turned over Byron's passport. Byron remained in jail while relatives worked to raise the bail money.

When I got home, Chrissy asked me how the hearing had gone.

"Not good. The judge lowered his bail."

Chrissy looked worried. "Do you think he's going to get out of jail?"

"I don't know, but there is a chance he could."

Chrissy was upset. "I don't need this kind of stress right now. I really don't."

The next morning, I was at the office and one of the correctional officers came and told me that a family member of Smith's had come to the jail with $50,000 cash to post bail for Byron. Byron was released just before 10:30 a.m.

"Please tell me you're joking," I said.

"No, it's true. I thought I better come and let you know."

I told him I appreciated the heads up. I meant it. I sat at my desk wondering how I was going to break this news to Chrissy. It was possible she'd hear about it on the news before I even got home from work. Either way, I knew it was not going to be good.

When I got home, Chrissy had already heard the news about Byron being released from jail. I asked her who she heard it from.

"It was all over the news. Now what do we do?"

I gave her a hug and said, "Don't worry. Things will be fine. I told Jamie and asked my coworkers to help keep an eye on our place. They'll be driving by our house constantly." From the expression on Chrissy's face, I could tell my words weren't offering too much comfort.

AUTOPSY REPORTS

Dr. Kelly Mills of the Ramsey County Medical Examiner's Office conducted the autopsies on the bodies of Nicholas Brady and Hailey Kifer on 11-24-2012. When the autopsies were completed, a final autopsy protocol report was sent to our office for evidence and review. It normally took a few weeks to get the report because the medical examiner had to wait for the laboratory results on the blood and urine tests.

The report on Nicholas Brady showed that he had a total of three gunshot wounds. The list of the wounds does not necessarily reflect the order in which he received them. They were listed as:

Gunshot wound #1. Entrance wound, back of right hand. Gunpower stippling on the skin surrounding wound. Wound tract, soft tissue and bone of the hand. Exit wound, palm of the right hand.

Re-entry wound, right temple of the head. Pseudostippling/abrasions, contusions, and lacerations on the skin surrounding the re-entry wound. Wound tract, skull and brain. Associated injuries, subgaleal hemorrhage, subarachnoid hemorrhage, lacerations of the brain, and fractures of the skull. Direction of the wound tract, slightly front to back, right to left, and straight. Jacketed bullet fragment recovered from the brain and retained. [*Final shot while lying wounded at the bottom of the stairs. 14mm rifle.*]

Gunshot wound #2. Entrance wound, left thumb. No evidence of close-range firing. Wound tract, soft tissue of the thumb.

Re-entry wound, left side of the abdomen. Wound tract, soft tissue of the abdomen, liver, and right lateral chest wall. Associated injuries, hemoperitoneum. Direction of the wound tract, front to back, left to right, and slightly upward. Bullet fragments recovered from the right lateral chest wall and abdominal wall. [*Shot while walking down the stairs. 14mm rifle.*]

Gunshot wound #3. Entrance wound, left side of the back. No evidence of close-range firing. Wound tract, soft tissue of the back, left posterior/lateral chest wall, left lower lobe of the lung, soft tissue of the back, and spinous processes of the thoracic spine. Associated injuries, hemothorax.

Exit wound, right side of the back. Direction of the wound tract, slightly front to back, left to right, and slightly downward. No bullet or fragments recovered from the wound tract. [*Shot while walking down the stairs. 14mm rifle.*]

Laboratory blood and urine test results show no alcohol or drugs in the system.

The report on Haile Kifer shows that she had a total of six
gunshot wounds. This is a list of the gunshot wounds, but
again, the shots didn't necessarily occur in this order.

Gunshot wound #1. Entrance wound, left side of
the face/left eye. No evidence of close-range firing.
Wound tract, soft tissue of the face, left eye socket,
and internal facial bones. Associated injuries, con-
tusion of the left eye. Direction of the wound tract,
front to back, left to right, and slightly downward.
Minute gilded, bullet fragment recovered from the
neck after dissection and searching. [*Shot while lying
wounded at the bottom of the stairs. .22 caliber pistol.*]

Gunshot wound #2. Entrance wound, behind left ear.
Charring of skin edges. No soot or gunpowder stippling on the skin surrounding wound. Wound tract,
soft tissue, skull, brainstem, and brain. Direction of
the wound tract, slightly front to back, left to right,
and slightly upward. Multiple gilded fragments recovered from the various location of the brain. [*Final
shot in the back-office workroom. .22 caliber pistol.*]

Gunshot wound #3. Entrance wound, right side of
the neck. Soot on the skin surrounding the wound.
Wound tract, soft tissue of the neck, soft tissue over-
lying cervical spine, left tonsil, and soft tissue near
the right temporomandibular joint/jaw. Direction of
the wound tract, front to back, right to left, and up-

ward. Multiple gilded fragments recovered from various locations of the neck and jaw. [*Shot while lying wounded at the bottom of the stairs. .22 caliber pistol.*]

Gunshot wound #4. Entrance wound, left side of the abdomen. Gunpowder stippling and unburned gunpowder flakes on the skin surrounding the wound. Wound tract, soft tissue of the abdomen, liver, and right hemidiaphragm. Associated injuries, hemoperitoneum. Direction of wound tract, front to back, left to right, and slightly upward. Gilded small-caliber bullet recovered from the right posterior chest wall and retained. [*Shot while lying wounded at the bottom of the stairs. .22 caliber pistol.*]

Gunshot wound #5. Entrance wound, back of the left forearm. No evidence of close-range firing. Wound tract, soft tissue of the forearm only. Exit wound, front of the left upper arm. Associated injuries, laceration of the left forearm.

Re-entry wound, left lateral thorax. Wound tract, left lateral chest wall, left lower lobe of the lung, and left posterior chest wall. Associated injuries, left hemothorax. Direction of the wound tract, slightly front to back, left to right, and slightly upward. Minute bullet core fragment and separate jacket recovered from the left posterior chest wall and retained. [*Shot while walking down the stairs. 14 mm rifle.*]

Gunshot wound #6. Entrance wound, right thumb. Soot on the skin surrounding the wound. Wound tract, skin, and soft tissue of the right thumb only. No bullet or bullet fragments recovered from the wound tract. [*Shot while lying wounded at the bottom of the stairs. .22 caliber pistol.*]

Laboratory blood and urine test results show no alcohol in the system, but it was positive for dextromethorphan and THC metabolite.

Dextromethorphan is found in cough syrup and is commonly abused by teenagers to get high. THC is found in marijuana.

After reviewing the autopsy reports and the statements he gave me, listening to the audio recording Byron made, and watching the surveillance video, there was only one conclusion I could make: Byron had no intention of catching someone; he was intent on murdering them.

I wondered if a jury would come to that same conclusion. I did not think Nick and Haile were innocent parties in this matter—absolutely not. But I do believe their actions were the lesser of the two evils.

I believe Satan is the father of lies, the master of manipulation, and the king of evil deeds. I thought he must have been very pleased with himself. He'd been successful in manipulating Nick and Haile's lust and greed for material possessions. And he fueled the fire of Byron's fear and anger.

After all the terrible acts I've encountered in my seventeen years as a deputy, I've come to believe there is an evil, dark force at work in this world. An evil, hell-bent on the destruction of mankind. I pray often that things will get better. Unfortunately, I see things getting worse.

I'm grateful that the number of good people I encounter outweighs the bad. I shudder to think what would happen if the scale tipped in the opposite direction.

DIVIDED COMMUNITY

As the days and weeks passed, the coffee-clutch conversation remained the same. Every day it was still Byron Smith. I heard about him everywhere, even at the local businesses I frequented such as Coborn's Grocery, Walmart, the Legion Club, and my dad's business, Luberts Auto Parts and Machine Shop.

There were a lot of people in the community who thought Byron was guilty, and seemingly just as many who thought he was innocent. And that wasn't just in Little Falls. It was throughout the county. It appeared the case had divided our community.

My dad, Greg, told me a lot of his customers came into his store to talk about the case. He noticed the community appeared to be divided. He said he got asked questions about the case all the time. "People think I know something because you're my son, but I don't, because you never told me anything."

"Dad, I can't talk to you or anyone else outside of my work about the case. I haven't even told Chrissy anything about the case."

"That's good, and I really don't want to know. This way when people ask me, I can honestly tell them I don't know anything."

"The next time someone asks you questions, just tell them to ask me. I'm fine telling people I can't talk about it."

I'd heard that friends of Byron who were his close neighbors, William Anderson and John and Kathleen Lange, had been allowing Byron to stay at their homes after he was bailed out of jail. I guess I couldn't blame Byron for not wanting to stay in his own house. I know I wouldn't want to after what had happened there. I don't believe in ghosts, but I also wouldn't want to tempt fate.

My great uncle lived near the Lange residence and was friends with John. John often showed up in the mornings at our coffee clutch because my great uncle was usually there. John had made it known that he and William Anderson were on Byron's side.

My friends and other family members who were present asked me what I thought about that.

"I really don't care. Everyone has the right to their opinion. There is a lot the public doesn't know right now that will come out in the trial."

"Like what?" they asked.

"You will have to wait and see."

Chrissy told me she'd noticed coworkers, friends, and family members of hers were similarly divided about what they thought of the case.

The news media had gone around the community asking residents what they thought, and they had reported in newspapers and on television that our community was divided over it.

You can't imagine how hard it was to keep a secret like this. Especially when I have people mad at me because I was the one who arrested Byron. It was a true test for me, but I was bound and determined to live up to my oath as a public servant. I know Jamie felt the same way.

Jamie and I live our lives knowing we are constantly in the public's eye. Everything we do is publically scrutinized, whether we do it on the job or in our private lives. That's a heavy burden to carry, but that's also one of the things that makes law enforcement officers special: we are willing to carry that burden.

WASHINGTON COUNTY ATTORNEY

Brian Middendorf called. "I need to meet with you regarding a troubling matter."

"I'll be upstairs as soon as I can," I told him.

When I got to his office, Brian said, "The Attorney General's Office is refusing to take over the prosecution of the Smith case. I figured I'd tell you in person since you're the lead investigator."

"Why are they refusing?" I couldn't believe what I was hearing.

"I don't know for sure, but I suspect the case might be too political of a matter for the attorney general to get involved."

"Have you told Sheriff Wetzel about this?"

"I talked with him before I called you."

"Do they see any problems with the case?"

"No. It's a good case. That's why it doesn't make any sense to me."

"So, what do we do now?"

"I put an email out to other county attorneys in the state. I'm waiting to hear back. I'll let you know what I figure out."

A couple weeks went by, and I had to drop some paperwork off at the county attorney's office. I was curious how things were going, so I met with Brian to see if they had figured anything out yet.

"I received a response from Washington County Attorney Peter Orput. I just got off the phone with him and he agreed to take the case. He's an extremely good attorney and has lots of experience prosecuting murder cases."

"That's awesome news. I look forward to meeting him."

Months went by, and then, one day while working at the office, I received a call from dispatch telling me the Washington County Attorney Peter Orput was in the front lobby and wanted to meet with me.

When I entered the lobby, I saw a tall, skinny, buck-toothed, middle-aged man wearing a suit and tie. My first impression was that he looked like someone from the *Revenge of the Nerds* movie.

"You must be Jeremy. Nice to meet you." He stuck out his hand and I shook it. I told him it was nice to meet him too. Peter then said, "I reviewed this case and was very impressed with the work you've done. I believe that Nick and Haile's deaths were murders, and I'm going to prove it to a jury."

"Thanks. Whatever you need from me, just ask. I'm here to help."

Peter asked me if there was a place he could go have a cigarette. I was glad he asked, because I was ready for one too. We walked out the front door to a designated smoking spot near our jail intake garage. As we stood there chatting and smoking, Peter said, "I've been trying to quit smoking, but I've been failing miserably."

"Well, you know, nobody likes a quitter."

Peter laughed and said, "I like your attitude."

As we stood outside, polluting our lungs, Peter told me about some of the interesting murder cases he'd prosecuted, and I told him about some of the bizarre cases I'd investigated. Peter's attitude and friendly demeanor made him very easy to like and get along with. Our attitudes seem to mesh well together, and I could feel that this was the start of a great working relationship.

"So, why would you volunteer to take on a case like this?" I asked him.

"I was upset when I saw the attorney general refuse to take the case. It's their job to help smaller counties that don't have the budget and manpower to handle these big cases. So, I contacted Brian and asked to review the case and see if I could help."

"I lost a lot of respect for the attorney general's office after Brian told me they refused to help."

"Yes, me too."

I was pleasantly surprised that my first impression of Peter was wrong. I mean, he still looked like a nerd, but he sure didn't act like one.

GRAND JURY HEARING

A year went by, and Smith's grand jury hearing was finally approaching. It was scheduled to take place on Tuesday, April 23, 2013. I was starting to get nervous and excited. I'd never had to testify in a grand jury hearing before.

In Minnesota, a grand jury can include up to twenty-three people, though they can function with as few as sixteen. A grand jury must be convened in cases in which the offense charged is punishable by life imprisonment. One of the important differences between a grand jury and a trial jury is that a grand jury hears from only one side: the prosecutor.

Criminal defense attorneys are not directly part of the grand jury process.

Prosecutors can also subpoena witnesses, who then must testify under oath to the jurors.

In this proceeding, the prosecutor presents evidence to the grand jury to establish there is probable cause to believe an offense has been committed, and that the defendant committed it.

Witness testimony consists of answering questions posed by the prosecutor and by the jurors.

After the grand jury hears the evidence, jurors vote on the indictments presented by the prosecutor. If at least twelve jurors vote that evidence establishes probable cause, an indictment is issued.

I had testified in plenty of felony cases. Too many to mention. But I had never testified in such a high-profile case.

I'd come to enjoy testifying in court. I got nervous, every time, in fact. But it got better every time I took the witness stand. It was like interviewing someone. The more I did it, the better I got. In my opinion, experience is the foundation of what makes a good officer great.

I studied my cases very carefully before I testified. I wanted to answer every question the attorney threw at me with accuracy and honesty.

I felt it was extremely important to maintain a calm demeanor and portray myself as confident and professional. I never wanted to raise my voice or get rattled under the pressure. The defense attorney could do that. I thought it made them look like an ass whenever they did it, but I also understood their need to put on a good show for their clients.

April 23 came, and I was fully prepared to testify. I was sitting on a bench in the hallway outside the courtroom patiently waiting my turn. Peter Orput came out of the courtroom and asked me to come inside. As you can imagine, the butterflies in my stomach started working overtime.

As I walked into the courtroom, the twenty-three-panel jury stared at me. I was asked to take the witness stand. It kind of gave me the willies because everyone was watching my every move. It was a closed hearing to the public, so the only people present in the courtroom were me, the jurors, the prosecutors, and the court transcriptionist. No one else was allowed inside.

Then the grand jury foreperson was asked to swear me in. "You do swear that the testimony you give here will be the truth, and nothing but the truth, so help you God?"

My answer, of course, was, "Yes, I do."

Orput has an assistant, Brent Wartner, who works with him. Orput informed the grand jurors that Wartner would be asking me the questions.

Wartner first had me describe my job title, occupation, and what my duties were. When I finished, he then asked me to describe what happened on November 23, 2012, the day I was called to Smith's residence.

I described in detail what I had walked into that fateful day at Smith's residence. Occasionally, I would glance over at the jury members while I was talking just to see their reactions. All of them appeared to be intensely interested in what I was saying.

Wartner had me talk until the point when I was ready to tell the jurors about the interviews I had with Smith at the sheriff's office. Instead of Wartner having me describe those interviews, he played all three audio interviews to the jury. The jury was also given the typed transcripts of the interviews to follow along with the audio. I was grateful he did that, because it would have been difficult for me to remember so many details.

It took a little over an hour and a half for the jury to listen to all three interviews. I had to sit on the witness stand while they listened. Halfway into it, my back started aching from the bulletproof vest I was wearing. I just sat there, trying my best to look professional until it was over.

When the interviews were completed, Wartner then

showed me and the jurors an aerial photograph of the depiction of where Smith's vehicle was located on Oak Lane, where Smith's residence is on Elm Street, and where Brady's vehicle was parked along Smith Avenue.

He handed me a laser pointer and asked me to highlight where Smith's residence was. I took the laser pointer and put the red dot on the house. He then asked me to highlight where Smith's vehicle was parked. I then put the red dot on Oak Lane, where his vehicle was parked. Then he finally had me highlight where Brady's vehicle was parked. I then put the red dot on Smith Avenue near the intersection of Riverwood drive.

When that was completed, Wartner said, "Mr. Foreperson. We are done with our examination of Sergeant Luberts. I will now open it to questions from you and the grand jurors."

The foreperson said he had no questions. Then some of the other juror members had questions.

Question: You made reference earlier when we were discussing the setup of the basement, and you said this chair seemed somewhat out of place. Did it appear as though all of the furniture had been moved or just possibly that chair?

Answer: No. What I meant is that it appeared, the way the chair was positioned and with the book shelving around it, it just seemed odd, like it was almost like a hiding spot, is what I meant by that.

Question: You referenced that he said, and he said this in the transcript, as well, that he read a lot from that chair. Did that environment seem conducive to a lot of reading, being a basement? Was it well lit?

Answer: I do not believe it was well lit and really not a very decent spot to read a book, because the light bulbs had been removed from the ceiling nearby.

Question: At any time when you spoke with him, did he indicate any names, other than what I believe were his neighbor's names and or reference to his neighbor?

Answer: From what I recalled, basically, he referred to the female many times, as you heard. And the female, each time he talked about her to me, basically meant Ashley Williams, which was his neighbor, right next door.

Question: Did he give you any indication that he realized that was not Ashley Williams lying on his floor?

Answer: No. In fact, the entire time that is who he thought it was.

Question: The two children that were in the basement, have you guys seen any prior problems with these two children throughout the town, or has it been reported through the sheriff's department? I mean, have they been seen or caught doing vandalizations of people's property, or have they been involved with the police department prior to this that you know of?

Answer: Not that I am fully aware of. (It should be noted that I understood this question as meaning before we found the children in Smith's home.)

Question: Is there anything that led you to believe . . . and maybe you can't answer this . . . that moving the pickup was a setup?

Answer: I would love to answer that. I very much believe that was part of the setup, yes.

Question: The first one, where he mentioned prior that the clothes were stolen, it almost sounded like it was Ashley that he was blaming. I was trying to wonder how long ago that was and what age she would have been. Would she have been a young kid that could have gone after him or something for some reason?

Answer: That is a good question, and I was not able to exactly determine it myself, because he referred to, yes, he referred to her taking this jacket from a theft from his place that occurred years ago. But I was unable to determine exactly how old she was at the time . . . or basically any time frame on it, but just that it happened a while ago.

Question: I was wondering, I noticed that Smith talked to Anderson, saying that the owner of the household had drinking problems. Have you had any problems with him, like, with anything with police activity or jail time or anything?

Answer: I personally have not.

Question: Now, on one of the earlier paper documents, I believe you said that when Haile came into the house she called out for Nick. Did he ever say that to you?

Answer: He did not. No, he did not.

After the jurors completed their questions for me, I was told I could step down. I then exited the courtroom, and they called in their next witness: one of the BCA agents. I was not allowed to sit in on any of the other testimonies.

I thought the hearing went very well for me. It was an experience I will never forget.

On April 24, 2013, the Morrison County grand jury handed down the sealed indictment for two counts of first-degree premeditated murder. That meant the case would go to trial in front of a twelve-panel jury. If Smith was found guilty of first-degree murder, he could get life in prison without parole.

An initial court appearance on the indictment was held in front of Judge Douglas Anderson the next day on April 25.

Orput requested that bail be set at $2 million given the nature of the offense and the possible penalties involved.

Judge Anderson kept the bail at $50,000 with conditions. Smith had already posted this bail so would remain out of jail until his criminal trial was completed and his fate was decided.

Smith's criminal charges had been enhanced from two counts of second-degree murder to two counts of first-degree murder, and still the judge had not increased his bail.

Frankly, I didn't understand that rationale of thinking. It always seemed law enforcement was fighting an uphill battle. The criminals often appeared to have more rights than the victims. I guess it really did go to show that people are presumed innocent until proven guilty in a court of law.

If that was Judge Anderson's thinking, I truly could not fault him for his decision. It was the right thing to do.

I've come to learn from my years of working in the public spotlight, it's a damned-if-you-do, damned-if-you-don't situation. No matter what, you are going to get criticized for your actions.

STRANGE ACTIVITY

Weeks, then months, passed by, and things were not getting any better at home. Chrissy told me she kept seeing strange vehicles, cars and trucks she had never seen before, driving past our residence. The drivers stared at our place as they drove by. I noticed the same activity.

Chrissy told me she was creeped out, and I must admit it was unnerving for me too.

Jamie and I noticed William Anderson and John Lange constantly driving slowly past our residences. We never noticed them driving by our houses before.

I was getting strange friend requests on Facebook from people I did not know.

I started to suspect Jamie and I were becoming targets of interest for people working on the defense of Byron Smith.

I shut down my Facebook account and got off all social media.

One evening when I got off work, I was sitting in the living room, looking out the window. I was looking across the street and saw a car parked in the alley behind my neighbor's house. I could see a male sitting behind the wheel with a pair of binoculars in his hands, staring toward my house. It looked to me like a private investigator was hired to watch me.

When I was a road deputy, I was called to respond quite often to situations such as this. People would call in a suspicious activity complaint.

I would respond, make contact with the vehicle, and talk with the driver. Most of the time, I would discover that's exactly what it was. A private investigator hired to watch a house. I would simply tell the driver that their cover had been blown because the homeowner spotted them. They would normally leave the area after being discovered.

I closed my window shades, then called my dispatch and asked them to send a local Little Falls Police Department squad to check it out. I watched as a squad car approached the suspicious vehicle in the alley. I saw the officer approach the driver and have a conversation with him. When the conversation was over, the vehicle drove away.

The officer called to tell me what he discovered. As I suspected, it was a private investigator who told him he was watching a residence.

I told Jamie about the incident, and he told me he had seen the same vehicle parked in the same alley on different days.

After that, I strongly suspected that Smith's defense team and friends were trying to catch my brother and I doing something wrong so they could use it against us during Smith's upcoming criminal trial.

About the only thing they were succeeding at was making me and my family's life miserable. As far as I knew, that might have been their only intention.

Jamie and I could have returned the favor and started harassing them, but that's not who we were. We refused to lower ourselves to their level.

A section in the Lord's prayer tells us, "As we forgive those who trespassed against us." Many people say these words, but don't really consider what they mean. I've thought a lot about these words, and I use them as a pillar in my life.

I would rather turn the other cheek than hold a grudge or take revenge. I'm quick to forgive. But I do not forget.

The way I see it, everyone will die someday, and we will all be judged in the end. A person might get away with something sinful in this life. But they won't get away with it in the next. So, why not try to make amends in this life before it's too late?

Like I said earlier, it's hard not to judge people. But my faith tells me not to. I believe in the end, someone much wiser than me will be doing the judging.

OMNIBUS HEARING

In August 2013, an omnibus hearing was set in Smith's case. It was to be held on August 30.

Under Minnesota State law, Rule 11, an omnibus hearing had to be held in felony and gross misdemeanor cases if the defendant pled not guilty. The omnibus hearing had to be held in the district where the alleged offense occurred.

The scope of the hearing is conveyed as: if the prosecutor or defendant demands a hearing, the court must conduct an omnibus hearing and hear all motions relating to:

a. Probable cause.
b. Evidentiary issues.
c. Discovery.
d. Admissibility of other crimes, wrong or bad acts.
e. Admissibility of relationship evidence.
f. Admissibility of prior sexual conduct.
g. Constitutional issues.
h. Procedural issues.
i. Aggravated sentence.
j. Any other issues relating to a fair and expeditious trial.

General procedures: The court may receive evidence offered by the prosecutor or defendant on any omnibus issue. A party may cross-examine any witness called by any other party.

Before or during the omnibus hearing or any other pretrial hearing, witnesses may be sequestered or excluded from the courtroom.

Omnibus motions: Probable cause motions: The court must determine whether probable cause exists to believe that an offense has been committed and that the defendant committed it.

The prosecutor and defendant may offer evidence at the probable cause hearing.

The court may find probable cause based on the complaint or the entire record, including reliable hearsay.

Aggravated sentence: If the prosecutor gave notice of intent to seek an aggravated sentence, the court must determine whether the law and proffered evidence support an aggravated sentence. The court must also determine whether to conduct a unitary or bifurcated trial.

In deciding whether to bifurcate, the court must determine whether the evidence supporting an aggravated sentence is otherwise admissible in the guilt phase of trial and whether a unitary trial would unfairly prejudice the defendant. The court must order a bifurcated trial if the evidence supporting an aggravated sentence includes evidence otherwise inadmissible at the guilt phase of the trial or if that evidence would unfairly prejudice the defendant in the guilt phase.

If the court orders a unitary trial, the court may order separate final arguments on the issues of guilt and the aggravated sentence.

Pretrial conference: The omnibus hearing may also include a pretrial conference to determine whether the case can be resolved before trial.

Continuances: The court may continue the hearing or any part of the hearing for good cause related to the case.

Determination of issues: The court must make findings and determinations on the omnibus issues in writing or on the record within thirty days of the issues being taken under advisement.

Pleas: The defendant may enter a plea to the charged offense or to a lesser included offense as permitted any time after the commencement of the omnibus hearing.

Entry of a plea other than guilty does not waive any jurisdictional or other issue raised for determination in the omnibus hearing.

Trial date: If the defendant enters a plea other than guilty, a trial date must be set.

A defendant must be tried as soon as possible after entry of a plea other than guilty. On demand of any party after entry of such plea, the trial must start within sixty days unless the court finds good cause for a later trial date.

Unless exigent circumstances exist, if trial does not start within 120 days from the date the plea other than guilty is entered and the demand is made, the defendant must be released under any nonmonetary conditions the court orders.

Omnibus hearings are open to the public.

Peter Orput told me I should expect the defense to ask me questions about the search warrants and statements. Their main goal was to try to get them thrown out as evidence.

"They will probably also try to get any statements or comments Smith made to you prior to his arrest stricken from the record."

"Do you see any issues or problems regarding this matter?"

"No. Everything looks rock solid to me."

"Smith didn't by chance decide to plead guilty yet, did he?"

Peter laughed and said, "Ah, no."

August 30 came and again it was time for me to testify. I sat on the witness stand and stared across the courtroom in front of me. Peter Orput and Brent Wartner were seated at the prosecutors' table to my right and Byron Smith, Steven Meshbesher, and his assistant, Adam Johnson, were seated at the defendants' table to my left.

It was the defense's time to question me regarding the work I had done on the case. The pressure was enormous. Everything I said could make the difference between evidence being admitted or thrown out of the case.

Judge Douglas Anderson told Meshbesher he could begin. Meshbesher told the court that his assistant, Adam Johnson, was going to do the examination on the witness.

Johnson had a book of questions for me. It took him about an hour to get through them all. At least, that's what it felt like.

Johnson did his best to try to trip me up, but I felt I held my own against him. Defense attorneys sometimes ask long, drawn-out questions. One trick I'd learned was to ask, "Can you please repeat that?" They look at me like I must be kidding them, since it puts the pressure back on them to have to repeat their long question. Some defense attorneys forget what they said and must abandon the question altogether.

I used that line on Johnson a few times. I give him credit, though, because he handled it like a pro and was able to re-ask the question.

Johnson kept circling back around to some of the same questions I had already answered, hoping to trip me up and get a disparate answer from me. I figured turnabout was fair play.

Peter was right about the defense asking me questions regarding the statements I obtained from Smith. The Miranda warning became a main topic during this line of questioning. It was a good thing I was adamant about using it each time I took a statement from Byron.

He was also right about the defense asking me questions about the search warrants. Luckily, I've had a lot of experience drafting and executing search warrants.

If the statements got thrown out, we would lose everything Byron admitted to me. And if the search warrants got thrown out, we would lose the digital audio recording we found above his reading chair and the surveillance video recording. That would be a major blow to our case. It wouldn't be worth bringing the case to a jury trial if that happened.

When Johnson completed his questions for me, it was Orput's turn to do a cross-examination. Orput asked me questions to clarify some of the questions Johnson had asked me, and the answers I had given to those questions. He also asked some questions that cinched up important facts.

When Orput completed his questions, he then had me confirm that a CD of all three audio statements I obtained from Smith was accurate. I had reviewed the CD that morning prior to court and could confirm it was accurate.

He then handed me copies of the typed transcripts from all three statements to confirm what was typed. Again, I reviewed this that morning before court and could confirm it was accurate.

The last items Orput showed me were all six search warrants and evidence receipts. I reviewed the forms and confirmed they were accurate.

I handed the items back to Orput and he then offered them as exhibits to the court. Judge Anderson asked Meshbesher and Johnson if there were any objections, and they said, "No, Your Honor."

That meant the judge would have access to the items and would review them to help him make his decision.

Orput and Johnson both had a few more questions for me, and when they completed their line of questioning, Judge Anderson told me I could step down.

I exited the courtroom feeling pretty good about how everything had gone. There were other officers needing to testify in the hearing, but I was excluded and not allowed to sit in on any of those testimonies.

During one of his breaks, Peter came down to the sheriff's office and asked if I wanted to have a smoke with him.

We went to our spot outside and I asked him what he thought of my testimony on the stand earlier that day.

"You did a really good job. I saw no issues in anything you said."

I was glad to hear that. I was kind of a perfectionist when it came to my job, and I hated making mistakes. On the other hand, I didn't mind criticism because I learned from my mistakes and seldom make the same mistake twice.

I asked him how the other officers were doing, and he said, "Good. You have a good team working this case."

"How long until you think Judge Anderson will give his ruling?"

"He has to make his decision within thirty days. Let's hope for the best. I'll call you as soon as I hear something."

Before the thirty days ended, Orput called me. He told me that Judge Anderson made a ruling regarding the omnibus hearing. I could tell that it was good news because he had some excitement in his voice.

"You did an awesome job. It all went in our favor. We didn't lose any evidence obtained in the case."

"Great job, Peter. Also, tell Brent great job from me, please."

Another huge burden had been lifted off my shoulders. After nearly a month of sleepless nights, I could finally breathe a little sigh of relief. I'm glad we didn't cause anything negative for the news media to talk about. They could focus their headlines on the upcoming jury trial instead of on our department.

THE CASTLE DOCTRINE

The news media had been on a mission to dramatize the castle doctrine. Although Minnesota does not have a stand-your-ground law, the state still applies the castle doctrine. This doctrine removes the duty to retreat if a person is threatened in his or her own home. Basically, Minnesota courts have decided that a person should not be required to retreat from his or her own home.

Self-defense in Minnesota is an affirmative defense against assault-based charges. Much of the analysis is tied to the reasonableness of the actions taken by the defendant and whether the defendant could have avoided the situation.

But if the defendant was in his or her house, there is no duty to retreat under the castle doctrine. A court of appeals case analyzed how far this castle doctrine extends.

First, there are four elements necessary for a successful self-defense claim.

1. The defendant was not an aggressor and did not provoke the alleged victim.

2. The defendant had an actual and honest belief of imminent danger.
3. A reasonable basis existed for this belief.
4. A reasonable means to retreat or otherwise avoid physical conflict were not available.

The fourth element is not required, though, when the defendant is in his or her home. The principle guiding the castle doctrine is that a person's home is his castle, his place of greatest safety. Therefore, the law does not expect or require a person to retreat from their home.

The court of appeals determined that the castle doctrine is limited to just the home and does not include the surroundings. But the duty to retreat only exists if and when there are reasonable means to do so.

As you can imagine, the reasonableness of actions in a self-defense case give way to much debate. That was certainly true in the Byron Smith case.

News media outlets were reporting that the decision to arrest Smith garnered national attention. Outraged gun-rights advocates felt the prosecution violated the castle doctrine and the rights of concealed carry permit holders to defend their homes.

On the other hand, while most experts, and the general public, agreed that forced-entry intruders present an imminent threat, they also believed there were limits to how much force should be considered reasonable to apply when defending one's property.

Sheriff Wetzel told news outlets during a press conference, "This isn't a case about whether you have the right to protect yourself in your home. You clearly do. That's a given. Rather, this is a case about where the limits are."

A twelve-panel jury would have to decide whether Byron Smith met three of the four elements necessary for a successful self-defense claim.

The question was whether the evidence we gathered in this case would be enough to prove beyond a reasonable doubt that Smith committed murder, or whether the castle doctrine would persuade concealed carry permit holders that Smith was legally defending his home.

Smith's jury trial was set to begin on April 21, 2014.

MOVING OUT

As the months went by, we were still being harassed by vehicles driving slowly past our house. I finally figured out why it was happening. Friends of Byron Smith started a coalition to help fund his legal defense. The group's meetings were held at the VFW in town. I found out that William Anderson and John Lange were active members. It appeared that someone had shared our addresses—mine and Jamie's—with the group. Whenever the meetings ended, we saw increased activity of vehicles driving by.

Chrissy was finally reaching her breaking point. The months of vehicles driving past and the comments people made to her had her rattled. It didn't help that the news media was making such a drama of everything.

"I just want to move out of town and get away from all this," she said one day.

I really didn't want to move away from my brother, but I felt I didn't have a choice. I could either stay and run the risk of losing my marriage or move and hope to save it. I never, in my wildest dreams, imagined this case would have such an impact on my life. In college and at cop training, they don't teach aspiring officers about the impacts a case can have on your personal life.

I was tired of my family being so affected in their own home. "Let's start looking at houses now, and in the meantime, we can put ours up for sale. It might take a while to sell."

I bought the house back in 2001 when I was a bachelor. It was the first house I'd ever owned. The realtor I worked with was Joel Larson, owner of the local business Riverside Realty. Joel was a good guy to work with. After that initial sale, I went to the house to move some things in. One of the things I brought with me was my cat.

Jamie was helping me move furniture. As we were working, we saw Joel pull up in his vehicle by the garage.

"I have an idea. Let's hide your cat in the cupboard in the hallway by the bedrooms and tell Joel to look and see what the previous owner left inside," Jamie said. I laughed and went along with his plan.

I grabbed my fat, fluffy, orange cat and put him in the cupboard. The cat had been my pal for the past five years and I didn't think he would mind helping me pull off this little prank.

The doorbell rang and I went to the door. When I opened it, Joel was standing on the back steps holding a case of beer in his hand. "I have a housewarming gift for you." He handed me the case of beer. I thanked him and asked him to come inside.

Jamie and I took a little break from our work to talk with Joel. As we were standing in the living room talking, Jamie said to Joel, "You should see what the previous owner left behind. I cannot believe they would do that." I kind of felt bad playing along with his prank after Joel's generosity, but

I just couldn't help myself. I blame Jamie's twin mind-melt for influencing me.

"Yeah, you've got to see this."

Jamie and I walked over to the cupboard between the bedrooms. Joel followed us. I then pointed to the cupboard door and said, "It's behind this door. Take a look." As soon as the door opened, Joel saw a big, fluffy, orange object with eyes staring back at him. Joel shuffled backward frantically and almost fell over.

Jamie and I laughed hysterically. When I finally caught my breath, I said, "That's just my cat."

"That was a first for me. After all the houses I've sold, no one has ever done that to me before. I almost shit myself when I saw that creature in the cupboard!" By that point, Joel was also laughing.

After a prank like that, I felt I owed it to Joel to hire him to sell my house. I mean, I'd almost given him a heart attack, for crying out loud.

I put a lot of time and tender loving care into that house. I knew I'd really miss it when I had to move.

Joel had his realtor sign posted in the front yard within a couple of days. Chrissy had been hard at work searching the internet for a new home.

Chrissy eventually found the home she liked. It was located about three miles east of town, off Skyview Ridge Road in Little Falls Township. The main thing was, it was out of town and away from the traffic that kept driving by our house.

We put an offer in on the house, and within a short period of time negotiating the price, our offer was accepted. Our current house still hadn't sold, but the bank agreed that we could afford both payments, so they gave us the loan for the new home. I figured if I had to, I could always rent my current home out to help make ends meet until it sold.

Smith's jury trial was a week away when we closed on our new home. Our new house had a huge living room and dining room with vaulted ceilings that needed to be repainted before we could move in. I was busy at work and barely had enough time to start moving, let alone paint.

Chrissy asked her parents if they would help with the painting. I was grateful for their help because I hate painting. When I got off work in the evenings, I ate supper, then helped paint until bedtime. Chrissy and I both had to work, so this routine went on into the time Smith's trial started.

THE JURY TRIAL

DAY 1

Monday, April 21, 2014 was the day Byron Smith's jury trial finally began. Local and national news media vans were parked outside the courthouse, and reporters lined the hallway. It was a sight to behold.

Peter Orput and Brent Wartner came to the sheriff's office a few days before to meet with me and the other officers who would be testifying. They wanted to go over our testimonies so that there were no surprises from us on the stand.

When I met with Peter, the poor guy looked like he'd aged ten years and hadn't slept in a month. His hair was sticking straight out to the side of his head.

"You look like hell. Are you okay?"

"To tell you the truth, it's been rough getting everything prepared. My nerves are getting the best of me right now."

"If you run into any problems during the trial, just let me know. If I can't help fix the problem, I'll find someone who can. If you need any moral support, someone to talk with, someone to have a cigarette with, come and get me. I'm here for you. You got this."

"Thank you. It's not often I run into someone this willing to help out. I really appreciate it."

Peter and Brent put aside their lives to come and help the residents of Morrison County. I figured offering my help in return was the least I could do.

On the day of the trial, Peter came into the sheriff's office to see me. "I need a cigarette before this fiasco begins."

I looked at him and said, "Let's go."

Peter looked much better than he had a couple of days ago. I was glad to see that. I could hear in his voice that he had his full confidence back. He was ready for this case.

A twelve-panel jury of six men and six women were picked, along with an alternate juror in case someone on the main jury had to be replaced for any reason. Deputy David Scherping would be the first person called to testify, and I was set to testify shortly after him.

Jurors heard opening statements from Peter Orput's assistant prosecutor, Brent Wartner.

Wartner said Smith's home had been burglarized multiple times and that Smith was angry about that. He told of how Smith had waited in his basement when Brady broke in, and again when Kifer followed him in, and shot them each multiple times, even though the first shot had wounded them. He told jurors their deaths were not reported to law enforcement until the following day, after Smith called his neighbor, William Anderson, who then dialed 911.

Meshbesher said, "This is not a case of 'whodunit.' Mr. Smith is the person who shot and killed those two people, but he is not criminally responsible for their deaths; he is not guilty of murder."

The prosecution then began presenting its case. Morrison County Deputy David Scherping was the first witness. He gave the jury the sequence of events that occurred after Anderson called law enforcement.

Then the mothers of the two dead teens, Kim Brady and Jenny Kifer, testified that they learned on November 23 that their children were dead. They told the jury their children's ages and identified photos of the teens.

After the mothers testified, it was my turn to testify. I was sitting downstairs in my office, going over the case and memorizing specific times, when the bailiff radioed to me that they were nearly ready for me. I walked upstairs past the news media cameras in the hallway and took a seat on the bench outside the courtroom.

It felt awkward because I had never had news cameras pointed at me prior to this case. It made me more nervous than I already was.

Within a short period of time, the bailiff came out and called me into the courtroom. As I walked in, I noticed the room was packed with news reporters. The court administrator stood up and asked me to raise my right hand. "You do swear that the testimony you are about to give is the truth, the whole truth, and nothing but the truth, so help you God?"

"I do."

"You may have a seat at the witness stand." I walked by the jury and sat down on the stand.

There was a brief pause as we waited for Judge Anderson to enter the courtroom. My nerves were starting to get the best of me and my legs were shaking a little bit. I looked out into the crowd and saw Sheriff Wetzel standing in the corner near the entry door. I said a little prayer to myself. "Please, God, don't let me make any mistakes."

I remembered being told I could calm my nerves by picturing everyone else naked. I stared into the crowd, trying to see if that would work. Sitting in front me were these beautiful female reporters, and I instantly knew that remedy would not work.

Judge Anderson then walked into the courtroom. The court administrator stood up and announced, "All rise." Everyone in the courtroom stood.

Judge Anderson then announced, "You may be seated. Mr. Orput, you may begin." Everyone in the courtroom took a seat and Orput began.

"Your Honor, my assistant Brent Wartner will be questioning this witness."

Judge Anderson told Wartner, "Mr. Wartner, you may begin."

Wartner started off with having me state my full name and date of birth for the record. He then had me state my job title and explain who I worked for and what I did. When that was completed, he asked me to explain what happened on November 23, 2012.

I started off by telling the jury I was off duty that day, at home with my family, when Deputy Scherping called and told me what William Anderson said. I recounted that I put my uniform on and drove to work to assist Deputy Scherping.

I told the jury that I met with Deputy Scherping and Deputy Mattison at the sheriff's office to plan what we would do, then we drove to Smith's residence to make contact with him. I told them that I made contact with William Anderson at the end of his driveway while en route to Smith's residence and confirmed with him what he had told Deputy Scherping.

Wartner then asked me what happened after that. I went on to describe what Deputy Scherping and I encountered after we drove up to Smith's house. I stated specific times in my details because I had memorized them beforehand. I was glad I did, because it seemed to impress the jury members. Both Orput and Wartner also looked impressed.

When I got to the part when I was ready to interview Smith, Wartner stopped me and said he was going to play the audio statements I took from Smith for the jury. Again, I was relieved he did that.

I spent another hour and a half sitting on the witness stand, watching the jury members look at the typed transcripts of the statements, listening to my interview with Smith. This time wasn't quite as boring, because I was looking out into the crowd and studying the jurors for their reactions.

When the jury was done listening to the statements, Wartner had a couple more questions for me. Then it was the defense's turn to cross-examine me.

I was very surprised that Meshbesher only had a few simple questions for me. I was expecting to be bombarded with questions, like during the omnibus hearing.

When Meshbesher was done asking his questions, I was told I could step down. As I was walking out of the courtroom, I noticed Sheriff Wetzel was no longer standing in the corner near the exit door.

I was in the hallway outside the courtroom when I heard Judge Anderson say they were going to be done for the day and reconvene the following morning.

I stood in the hallway until the courtroom cleared and Peter came out. Peter walked up to me and the first words out of his mouth were, "Let's go have a cigarette."

We walked outside to our usual spot by the jail intake garage. Peter told me, "Nice job in there today. I was impressed with your testimony and that you knew exact times."

"I studied. I must have reviewed my report a hundred times before today. Any idea why Meshbesher asked me hardly any questions?"

"Judge Anderson ruled before the trial started that the defense couldn't bring up anything about the juveniles and what they did."

"Why not?"

"Because this trial is about what Byron did. Not what Nick and Haile did."

When I finished talking with Orput, I walked to my office to finish my workday. As I sat down, I saw a letter lying on top of my desk. I glanced at the letter, and it said *Official Commendation*. It was signed by Sheriff Wetzel.

Dear Jeremy,

Please consider this an official commendation for your work on the Byron Smith homicide case. Your efforts at the crime scene, in the interview room, and finally in the courtroom, were all examples of first-rate police work. On a case with such notoriety, I feel extremely fortunate and proud to have had you as our lead investigator.

While it might be considered odd for me to issue this commendation prior to the resolution of the case, it is not an accident. While I am confident that Smith will be convicted of homicide, juries are strange things, and you never know for certain how they will vote until the very end. I deliberately issued this letter now because regardless of the jury's verdict, your work is deserving of recognition as the finest my office has to offer. Thank you for making our entire office look good throughout this entire case. This commendation is offered on behalf of my entire office and the grateful citizens of Morrison County.

Sincerely,

Sheriff Michel Wetzel

I couldn't believe my eyes. It was a huge honor to receive such a recognition from the sheriff. Now I knew why I hadn't seen him standing in the courtroom when I finished testifying.

I walked into his office and said, "Thank you, Michel, very much. I really appreciate this."

"You deserve it. Thank you for all you do."

When I got home from work, I showed the letter to Chrissy.

"This was very nice of Michel. It's good to see you were recognized for your hard work after all the hell you've been through."

As nice as it was to receive this commendation, I couldn't help but think of what Jesus told us: "Seek not the rewards of this life, for your greatest reward will be given to you in heaven."

CHAPTER
32

JURY TRIAL

DAY 2 & 3

Tuesday, April 22, 2014. As the second day of the trial began, the prosecution played the audio clip from the digital audio recorder found in the bookshelf above Smith's reading chair. I wish I could have been in the courtroom to see their reactions, especially the news media's reaction.

BCA Senior Special Agent Museus testified that he was on duty in Bemidji the day after the shootings on Nov. 23, 2012, when, at about 2 p.m., the Morrison County Sheriff's Office called for help. Museus said he arrived at the Smith residence about 5 p.m. or 6 p.m. and assisted the crime scene team in removing the bodies from the residence.

Museus told the jury that the audio clip they'd just heard was a taken from six hours of audio recovered. The audio recording had been discovered atop one of the two tall bookcases set up in Smith's basement.

The bookcases were arranged so that one was on either side of a cushioned chair where Smith was sitting when the break-in occurred. The furniture was stationed off to the side at the bottom of the basement steps.

In the afternoon, when BCA Forensics Specialist Nathaniel Pearlson testified, photos of were shown of Smith's home, including the broken window in his bedroom. Glass littered the dresser and the floor in the room. Other photos and diagrams showed the layout of Smith's home, and how the furniture was placed in Smith's basement.

A water jug and snack bars were on a table next to the chair and bookcases. Just off that room was the workshop, and a photo showed the body of Kifer lying atop the body of Brady, both wrapped in a tarp.

Pearlson showed the jury the two guns used in the shooting, the Ruger Mini-14 semi-automatic ranch rifle and the high-standard double-nine convertible .22 pistol capable of holding nine rounds.

He pointed out blood that was found under towels and rugs in Smith's basement, as well as blood on the wall next to the stairs and on a portion of the ceiling.

Pearlson also pointed out light bulbs that had been removed from three light fixtures and indicated the area where six light bulbs were found along with glass lampshades near the chair between the bookcases.

Pearlson testified about holes found in the hooded sweatshirt Kifer was wearing, noting that his conclusion on gun residue testing was that one of the shots had been taken within six inches of her.

During the defense's questioning of Pearlson, Meshbesher asked him about the patterns of residue found that would indicate how close a shot might be, and Pearlson explained how he could determine the range from which the gun was fired.

Pearlson told Meshbesher his report for the court contained the conclusions he had made while processing the evidence, and that the basis for the conclusions were in his notes.

Assistant Defense Attorney Adam Johnson called for a mistrial, saying the defense had not been provided with Pearlson's notes during discovery.

Assistant Prosecutor Brent Wartner countered that the state had provided all the evidence, and had even made available to the defense the opportunity to view evidence that was not in the state's possession, but was available through other agencies. The state was not required to carry it to them.

Pearlson said he had his roughly hundred pages of notes at the courthouse.

Judge Anderson denied the motion for mistrial but offered to provide copies of Pearlson's notes, as well as time for defense to talk to Pearlson about the notes before the jury was reconvened.

The defense also called for a mistrial because of Judge Anderson's prior ruling that cell phone calls on the teens' phones were inadmissible. Then they called for mistrial for comments the prosecutor had made to the media about convicting Smith.

Judge Anderson again denied the motions for mistrial.

Wednesday, April 23, 2014, was the third day of the trial. It began with Agent Pearlson's continued testimony. Pearlson was questioned by the defense on the layout of Smith's home, the blood found there, and the shell casings, holes, and gun residue found on the clothing of Brady and Kifer.

Pearlson said a metal bar found outside leaning against the wall beneath the broken window had been taken into evidence, but it had not been tested, a decision that was not his to make.

Pearlson also said a glass pipe found in Kifer's purse had not been tested for any sort of residue.

BCA Agent Janet Nelson then took the stand. Agent Nelson testified that she had analyzed the digital audio recorders recovered from Smith's basement.

Nelson told the jury about the audio recording that was discovered on the digital audio recorder found on the bookshelf above Smith's reading chair. She told the jury that because of the long pauses and empty spaces in the recording, she condensed the recording into approximately twenty-nine minutes of important audio.

Agent Nelson then testified about the video recording she recovered from Smith's video surveillance system. Orput played the surveillance video for the jury to watch during Nelson's testimony.

Agent Nelson explained to the jury that you can see Smith exit his front door, enter his vehicle, back it out, and leave at about 11:25 a.m. Nelson said when she turned on the DVR recorder, it was time stamped with the time and date of each video. She checked the accuracy with her own cell phone. "They were within seconds."

Smith returned to his home on foot twenty minutes later at about 11:45 a.m.

At 12:33 p.m., Brady is seen running up the stairs of the deck in the back of the residence. He begins looking in windows and tries a door. About 12:35 p.m. he spots a camera positioned in a wood pile and turns it upside down. On another camera, he can be seen holding his hands over his face. He's seen walking around the front of the house at about 12:37 p.m., and he goes around to the back of the house at about 12:38 p.m. At 12:39 p.m., he's seen for the last time on the surveillance video on the upper deck in the back of the house.

It's not until 12:51 p.m. that Kifer can be seen running across the driveway in the front yard to the upper deck. She's carrying a large pink purse and has a cell phone to her ear. She walks out of camera range and walks into another camera range at 12:53 p.m.

"That's the last either is seen on camera," Nelson said.

CHAPTER
33

JURY TRIAL

DAY FOUR & FIVE

On Thursday, April 24, 2014, Dr. Kelly Mills, medical examiner with the Ramsey County Medical Examiner's Office, took the stand. Mills performed autopsies on Brady and Kifer.

As Mills testified about the wounds found on each of the bodies during the initial autopsy, the prosecution projected large, graphic photos of the wounds that had been taken during the autopsy.

Mills started with Nicholas Brady and explained what she discovered as outlined in her autopsy report.

Mills said any one of the three shots to Brady could have been fatal after a certain amount of time, but that the gunshot that entered his brain was the first one to cause his death.

Mills said she used reports on the clothing of the deceased from the BCA, but to determine sequence of the gun firing, she listened to the audio to determine when Brady stopped making vocal patterns.

Based on that, Mills determined the gunshot that went into his brain was the final shot.

Mills then talked about Haile Kifer, again explaining what she discovered as outlined in her autopsy report.

During her testimony, Mills identified a gunshot wound by Kifer's left eye as a picture was projected onto a screen for the jury to see.

Mills said two different types of ammunition were used in the shots fired at Kifer.

Mills testified that the shot which was fatal to Kifer was a gunshot from close range, since charring occurs when a gun is very close to the skin surface. That bullet traveled through the soft tissue of Kifer's neck, a portion of the left tonsil, into the skull, where it damaged the brain stem and fractured into various portions of her brain, where Mills recovered multiple fragments.

Mills said the cause of death in both instances was "multiple gunshot wounds, homicide."

Defense attorney Steve Meshbesher questioned Mills about the meaning of the "homicide" as used in a cause of death report. Mills said in her line of work, the word "homicide" is made in reference to one human being killing another human being, not necessarily murder; it does not include intent, she said.

Meshbesher questioned Mills about determining whether a wound would have been fatal or non-fatal, whether a wound would incapacitate or fatally wound a person, and if it could be determined where on the stairs the person was when a certain shot was fired.

Mills said she could determine three shots were fired during the audio when Brady could be heard.

Meshbesher asked whether a person who had sustained

the first two gunshot wounds would have still been able to move. Mills said the two first gunshot wounds would not have disabled Brady to such a degree that he could not stand.

"Theoretically, Mr. Brady would have the ability to stand, although he would not be able to use his right hand."

Meshbesher asked whether, if Brady had a gun in his sweatshirt, he could have used a gun. Mills said theoretically he could have used his left hand.

Meshbesher further questioned if, after sustaining the first gunshot wounds, that person could still be violent, and whether that violence could be deadly, beyond control of the shooter. Mills said, "There is that possibility."

Mills confirmed Brady could have been moving around before the final gunshot and possibly in a violent way.

As for Kifer, Meshbesher asked about the six shots heard in the audio when she was shot.

Mills said she heard six shots fired in the audio and had to separate them. Meshbesher asked whether the sixth shot heard could have missed. Mills said, "That's possible, but six were fired and Kifer sustained six gunshot wounds."

Meshbesher asked whether the first gunshot wound sustained by Kifer incapacitated her and whether she would have still been able to move. Mills agreed Kifer would have been able to use three out of four of her limbs.

Mills was unable to verify the time lapse between the shots fired at Kifer, but admitted she did recall that she was aware that Smith had said he shot Kifer under the chin. That wound, determined to be the final wound, had soot.

Meshbesher said Kifer was heard making sounds on the audio recording and asked whether a deceased body can continue to make sounds. Mills said sounds could be from air coming from the body. She also testified that when a body is moved from side to side, a moaning sound could be heard.

Meshbesher asked whether it was possible that Mr. Smith heard a postmortem sound when he told law enforcement he heard noise from Kifer after the fifth shot. Mills said, "If he was moving her."

Dr. Mills, responding to Meshbesher, agreed that if a person had acted in self-defense, or in defense of home when shooting another, that manner of death would still be called "multiple gunshot wounds, homicide."

Dr. Mills said as for the toxicology report on Kifer, she was not able to determine how the marijuana metabolite was ingested or how recently.

Mills said that a person could die from abusing dextromethorphan, the other drug found in Kifer's system, and that Kifer would have been considered intoxicated by the amount in her system at the time of her death.

Mills verified the drug could cause hallucinations, alter perception, and possibly cause a psychotic effect in chronic abusers.

Smith's neighbor, William Anderson, was next to testify. He was questioned briefly about a visit he had with Smith the morning of Nov. 22, 2012, at 10:30 a.m. Anderson said he could not recall what Smith said about a female neighbor as she drove by.

The last to testify for the prosecution was BCA forensic scientist Brent Matzke. He provided information on DNA collected from items taken from the crime scene.

Matzke said that the blood of eighteen-year-old Haile Kifer was found on the barrel of Smith's revolver and on his pants.

When BCA Agent Matzke completed his testimony, the state then rested its case.

The jury was asked by Judge Anderson to leave the courtroom so the judge could have a brief bench consultation with the prosecution and defense. Meshbesher moved for acquittal. The state asked the court to deny the motion.

Judge Anderson denied the motion immediately.

After a brief meeting, the jury was called back in. The defense then began its case by cross-examination of my brother, Deputy Jamie Luberts.

Meshbesher asked Deputy Luberts about his investigation of an October 27, 2012, burglary of Smith's home.

Luberts said he was shown that the bottom panel of a basement walkout door had been kicked out. He was also shown areas of the home that someone had ransacked, including a dresser in Smith's bedroom. He had documented the scene with photos.

Luberts testified he did not collect fingerprints from the handle of the door, doorknobs, or dead bolt. Neither did he collect fingerprints from the outside screen door or the interior wooden door.

Luberts said it appeared that Smith's things had been gone through in several rooms of the house, both downstairs and upstairs.

In Smith's bedroom, Luberts said he removed a fingerprint from the top of the nightstand, but he later learned it was not sufficient quality to get a good print. It was still in evidence.

Luberts said a handprint on top of a wooden box had looked more like a smudge than a regular hand-down handprint, and he didn't believe there was enough detail to lift a print. He said he didn't make a judgement of whether it was a print from a bare hand or a gloved hand.

Luberts said Smith told him he had chained off the driveway as a response to the burglaries.

Luberts said he followed up with Smith twenty days after the reported burglary but had no leads on suspects in the burglary.

Judge Anderson then adjourned for the day. The trial would continue the following morning with more testimony from Deputy Luberts.

On Friday, April 25, 2014, Deputy Jamie Luberts retook the stand.

Meshbesher continued his line of questioning regarding the October 27, 2012, burglary Smith had reported.

Luberts said two days after receiving the report from Smith, Smith came to the sheriff's office and submitted a list of other stolen items including a camera lens, Nikon camera worth thousands of dollars, gold coins, cash, a gold ring, and a rifle scope.

Luberts testified he didn't develop any suspects in the case or check any pawn shops for the stolen merchandise.

Morrison County Sheriff Michel Wetzel was called to testify next. Sheriff Wetzel testified that on November 29, 2012, he learned where Smith's stolen shotgun may have been located. Wetzel met with someone who brought him to the gun's location. The gun was found at the end of a wooded trail in a swampy area, partially covered by grass and snow.

When Sheriff Wetzel concluded his testimony, Judge Anderson adjourned for the day.

JURY TRIAL

DAY 6

After a weekend away from the courtroom, the trial resumed on Monday, April 28, 2014. The defense called private investigator Ross Rolshoven to the stand. Rolshoven testified regarding his investigation following the shooting. He talked about a panel kicked out of Smith's basement door in an October 27, 2012, burglary and the subsequent footprint left on the panel.

The defense presented Nick Brady's shoes, which had been recovered from Smith's basement, but the prosecution objected to comparing the tread on Brady's shoes to the tread on the door, calling the connection irrelevant.

Judge Anderson ruled on a pre-trial motion regarding the shoe that the connection between the two burglaries was irrelevant. Anderson ruled that Smith didn't know who broke into his house previously, so he wouldn't know if the same people returned on Thanksgiving Day, 2012.

The defense called three character witnesses to the stand.

Byron's brother, Bruce Smith, testified about his younger brother's work with the Eagle Scouts and said Byron was "highly regarded by everyone that has known our family."

Prosecutor Orput asked Bruce if he had ever known anyone who had acted out of character before. Bruce said he had not.

Smith's neighbors, Kathleen Lange and her sixteen-year-old son, John Dillon Lange, each testified.

John Dillon Lange told the court he and his band were allowed to practice music in Smith's detached garage.

Lange also testified that Smith had lived at his parents' rural Little Falls home since the shootings occurred.

Meshbesher asked Lange about his opinion of Smith's reputation in the community and if he had a reputation for being honest. After several objections from the prosecution, Lange answered that he thought Smith was an honest person.

Orput asked Lange, "It's real known around here that you don't mess with that guy, isn't that true?"

Objections from the defense prevented Lange from answering and led Meshbesher to state the questioning was "absolutely improper."

"I'm asking for a mistrial." Judge Anderson denied Meshbesher's request for a mistrial.

Orput questioned Lange about practicing with his band in Smith's garage and asked if the band was kicked out.

Lange maintained that the band left on its own accord to practice at another location.

Kathleen Lange then took the stand and testified that Smith had lived in her home for the sixteen months since the shooting. She said, "I believe him to be very honest."

Smith made it clear to the judge and jury that he would

not testify in the case but would exercise his right to remain silent. The defense then rested their case.

Closing arguments were set for the following day.

Judge Anderson told the jury that Minnesota law allows people to use deadly force in self-defense if they fear death or great bodily harm, or to prevent a felony from being committed in one's dwelling. He said a defendant has no duty to retreat, but that a defendant's actions must have been reasonable under the circumstances. He also told them to follow the law as he explained it, even if they believed the law was or should be different.

Judge Anderson instructed the jury to pack overnight bags because they'd be sequestered until they reached a verdict. The court was then adjourned for the day.

Outside the courtroom, Meshbesher told the media his client had, in effect, already testified when he spoke to police.

"He was willing, he was wanting to do anything . . . he was taking my advice. When I reviewed this over the weekend . . . all he'd do is repeat what he already said," Meshbesher claimed.

JURY TRIAL

DAY SEVEN
"THE VERDICT"

On Tuesday, April 29, 2014, closing arguments started first thing in the morning. Peter Orput addressed the jury.

I was no longer needed to give testimony in the case, so I was allowed to sit in on the rest of the hearings. The courtroom was packed, of course, so I stood in the back corner with Sheriff Wetzel and watched.

"This is a very serious but simple case," Orput reasoned. Orput told the jury he believed there was evidence to prove Smith had a plan and a determination to kill seventeen-year-old Nick Brady and eighteen-year-old Haile Kifer. Orput said, "Every time Smith pulled the trigger, he had a choice to consider."

Orput said that at 10:30 a.m. on Thanksgiving Day, 2012, Smith met with his neighbor William Anderson. The two saw their neighbor Ashley Williams drive by. Orput said he believed that was when Smith decided to move his truck away from his house. Orput says Smith made sure there was a tarp nearby in the basement and activated his digital recorder.

Orput said evidence showed there was a bottle of water and snacks next to the chair along with a novel. Orput claimed this was evidence of Smith lying in wait. Orput said, "This sounds like deer hunting." He also asked the jury to consider whether sitting in the chair and waiting for Brady to come down the stairs was Smith's only option.

Orput played the audio recordings of the shooting again for the jury. During the presentation, Smith's hands were covering his face and he appeared to be crying.

The audio from after the shootings was also played for the court, and a transcript of the audio was displayed on a projector screen with a time reference to the shootings.

24 minutes before the shootings: "In your left eye."

18 minutes before the shootings: "Bruce, ah, stop tomorrow morning, no rush but as soon as convenient. Can you do that? Uh, park to the north 100 feet . . . no . . . 100 yards north of the corner and walk in from the west."

11 minutes before shootings: "I realize I don't have an appointment, but I would like to see one of the lawyers here."

Orput said that the audio was a rehearsal of what to say after the shootings.

56 minutes after shootings: "No rush, but ya know, as it's convenient for you."

57 minutes after shootings: "I left my house at 11:30.

They were both dead by 1."

1 hour 40 minutes after shootings: "I felt like I was cleaning up a mess. Worse than spilled food. Worse than vomit, worse than shit. Cleaning up a mess."

1 hour 40 minutes after shooting: "You're dead."

1 hour 42 minutes after shooting: "There was a major complication in my life. You really don't want to know. Believe me. You don't want to know."

1 hour 43 minutes after shootings: "I am not a bleeding-heart liberal. I felt like I was cleaning up a mess. Not like spilled food. Not like vomit. Not even like . . . not even like diarrhea. The worst mess possible. And I was stuck with it . . . in some tiny little respect . . . in some tiny little respect. I was doing my civic duty. If the law enforcement system couldn't handle it, I had to do it. I had to do it. The law system couldn't handle her and if it fell into my lap and she dropped her problem in my lap . . . and she threw her own problem in my face. And I had to clean it up."

1 hour 46 minutes after shootings: "I have not yet called the sheriff."

1 hour 46 minutes after shootings: "They weren't human. I don't see them as human. I see them as vermin, social mistakes. Social problems. I don't see them as . . . human. This bitch was going to go through her life, destroying things for other people.

Thieving, robbing, drug use."

4 hours 32 minutes after shootings: "Cool, exciting, highly profitable until someone kills you. It's begging to have him shoot me. That's like begging to have him shoot me. Yep . . . you should see the rugs on the basement floor."

4 hours 45 minutes after the shootings: "It's a sucker shot. People going down strange stairs naturally watch the steps. Like I give a damn who she is. Like I care who she is."

4 hours 56 minutes after shootings: "I'm sorry, so much regret. I try to be a good person. I try to do what I should. Be friendly to other people. Help them when I can. Try to be a good citizen. Not cheat people. Be fair. A bad family raises a bad person like this. And because I try to be a decent person, they think I'm a patsy. I'm a sucker. They think I'm there for them to take advantage of. Is that the reward for being a good person? And then they dump this mess on me. It's not a mess like spilled food. It's not a mess like vomit. It's not even a mess like diarrhea. It's far worse. Then they take slice after slice out of me."

4 hours 58 minutes after shootings: "Five thousand . . . five-thousand-dollar slice, ten-thousand-dollar slice. And if I gather enough evidence they might be prosecuted. If they are prosecuted, they might go to court. If it goes to court, they might be found guilty. If they are found guilty, they might

spend six months to two years in jail, and they're out. And they need money worse than ever, and they are filled with revenge. I cannot live like that. I can't have that chewing on me for the rest of my life. I cannot. I refuse to live with that level of fear in my life."

5 hours and 8 minutes after shootings: "She's tough, she's eye candy. It's games. It's exciting and it's highly profitable, until somebody kills you. Until you go too far, and somebody kills you. Until you go too far, and somebody kills you. Until you try to take advantage of somebody who is not a sucker, who is not a patsy."

5 hours and 22 minutes after shootings: "Mother and father are both semi-psychotic. I put even odds that one or the other will come over here with a gun."

Orput said, "Was it fear that drove this or something else? Anger. Resentment. Now it is your case. You know what happened. You know what his state of mind was. I'm asking you now to bring back just verdicts. That's all."

After Orput finished his closing arguments, it was the defense's turn.

In his closing argument, standing at a podium, Steven Meshbesher told the jury, "This is a case about courage."

Meshbesher said Brady and Kifer drove together and parked in a hidden location. The two got out of the car and were trespassing onto Smith's property.

Brady had a hood on his face and gloves on his hands. He used a steal rod to break a double-pane window. The defense brought a double-paned glass window into the courtroom for the jurors to see.

Meshbesher told the jury that homes are where people live to feel safe. He continued that Brady climbed into Smith's home through the window. Minutes later, after hearing three gunshots, Kifer crawled in through the same window.

The defense argued that the three gunshots should have warned her not to enter the home. They believed Kifer thought the shots came from Brady, which was why she went looking for him.

The defense said if the two teenagers wouldn't have committed a felony burglary, then they would still be alive today.

Meshbesher stated that Smith did not ask the teenagers to come over to his home; they came voluntarily. The defense reminded the jury that the state had the burden of proof.

Meshbesher did not believe that the state had enough evidence to convict Smith of the murder charges. He stated that there were no official records that indicated if the workshop phone was working in Smith's basement.

The phone was not analyzed or taken in as evidence. Meshbesher also stated the jury heard no audio regarding the light bulbs being unscrewed. The defense ended their final argument by thanking the jury and again stating that Smith was acting in self-defense and defending his dwelling.

The prosecution was allowed to rebuttal the defense's closing argument. During that time, Orput said the reason the metal pipe wasn't taken into evidence was because Brady had been wearing gloves. He also said it was unnecessary to take the workshop phone in as evidence because a BCA agent had made a phone call from the phone with witnesses present.

Judge Anderson then addressed the jury one final time before dismissing them for deliberation.

I waited in the hallway as the courtroom was clearing because I knew Orput had to be in desperate need of a cigarette. I knew I was.

Peter and I went to our usual spot and talked. Peter asked me how he did.

"Well, you could have smiled more and given a wink to some of the older ladies on the jury."

Peter laughed. "Smartass."

"All jokes aside, I don't think anyone could have done any better. Great job in there."

Peter asked me if I wanted to go for lunch with him and I said, "Absolutely. Let's walk upstairs and see if Wartner, Middendorf, and Kosovich want to join us." We went to the county attorney's office and met with them, then we all went to have lunch together.

The five of us walked over to Black and White, a restaurant located downtown about two blocks away.

When we got to the restaurant, I radioed my dispatch that I would be out of service for lunch. As we were sitting there talking, dispatch radioed me and asked if Orput was with me. I told them he was. Dispatch told me the jury had an important question they wanted to ask and needed to talk with Orput.

I told Orput, and he called the county attorney's office to find out what was going on.

A little while later, Orput got off the phone and told us, "The jury wanted to know if they convicted Smith on the first-degree murder charges, do they have to consider the second-degree murder charges."

Orput told us this could be a really good sign that the jury had already made up their minds to convict Smith.

The mood was very positive as the five of us sat and ate

our lunches. The restaurant was full of people, and I took a moment to look around me. I saw many familiar faces that I'd come to know growing up in this town. Some of the people stopped by our table and told us they saw us on the news and appreciated the work we were doing.

Those kind words coming from the people in my community made me proud to be a Little Falls native. Peter said, "You guys have some nice people in this community. You don't get this in the metro area."

I told him, "The advantages of living in a small town."

We finished having lunch and started walking back to the courthouse. Across the road from the restaurant, at the corner, was my dad's parts store. As we were walking, I told Peter, "To my left is my dad's parts store."

"Let's stop quick. I would like to go in and meet your dad." I was a little shocked that he wanted to take the time to do that.

We walked into the shop and my dad was standing behind the counter. I introduced Peter to my dad.

My dad and Peter really hit it off. I can't say I was surprised, since they both have the gift of gab. Peter told my dad, "I had to stop and meet Jeremy's dad. Your son did a great job in the Smith case and was a big help to me. You should be proud of him, he's a hard worker. I think I know where he gets it from."

My dad thanked Peter for the kind words and for taking the time to stop in and meet him. We then left the store and continued back to the courthouse.

I was amazed Peter took time out of his busy day to do that. It made me proud to know him and call him my friend.

A little over three hours into the jury's deliberation, they made a decision. I was in the sheriff's office when the call came into dispatch that the jury was ready to give their verdict. Sheriff Wetzel, a few other deputies, and I walked upstairs to provide courtroom security and listen to the decision.

When we got to the top of the stairs, the hallway leading to the courtroom was bustling with reporters who had obviously been notified that the jury had made a decision in the case.

I walked into the packed courtroom and stood in the corner near the exit door with Sheriff Wetzel so that we could keep an eye on everyone. This was a highly emotional case, and we didn't know how people would react.

Byron Smith and his legal team were seated at a table in front of us to our right, and Orput and Wartner were seated at the prosecutors' table to our left. Byron sat there in his suit and tie with a frown on his face, waiting to hear what his fate would be. Tension was so high in the courtroom, you could cut it with a knife.

A door opened and the jury walked in. A hush fell over the crowd as the jury members took their seats. Someone's cell phone started ringing. Everyone in the courtroom looked around to discover whose cell phone it was.

There is a sign posted on the wall outside the courtroom that says, "No cell phones or drinks allowed in the courtroom."

Byron's attorney, Meshbesher, turned his chair back toward the crowd of people with a disgusted look on his face. As everyone was looking into the crowd, we saw William Anderson reach into his pants pocket and pull out his ringing cell phone.

The courtroom bailiff walked over to Anderson and motioned for him to follow him. Anderson stood up and was escorted out of the courtroom. It must have been an embarrasing moment for him.

A short time later, Judge Anderson entered the courtroom. The court administrator announced, "All rise." Judge Anderson came in and took his seat. He then said, "You may be seated. Has the jury reach a decision?"

The jury foreperson said, "We have, Your Honor."

Judge Anderson said, "Please give your decision to the court administrator." The court administrator then handed the form to Judge Anderson for his review.

After Judge Anderson reviewed the form, he handed it back to the court administrator and the jury's decision was read.

I stood there feeling great anticipation, as I'm sure everyone else in the courtroom was feeling too. The two years of hard work and criticism I had endured was about to be finished.

"On the first count of murder in the first degree with premeditation regarding Nicholas Brady, we the jury find Byron Smith guilty as charged. On the second count of murder in the first degree with premeditation regarding Haile Kifer, we the jury find Byron Smith guilty as charged.

"On the third count of murder in the second degree regarding Nicholas Brady, we the jury find Byron Smith guilty as charged. On the fourth count of murder in the second degree regarding Haile Kifer, we the jury find Byron Smith guilty as charged."

I looked at Smith. He showed no emotion as the verdict was read.

I felt such enormous satisfaction and relief after hearing the verdict. I looked into the crowd seated in front of me and saw Brady's and Kifer's parents and family members crying. My heart went out to them. They were finally able to get some relief from all their grief.

The look on their faces was an assurance to me. It reminded me why I had chosen to be a law enforcement officer, and especially an investigator.

After the verdict was read, Judge Anderson thanked the jury for their service to the public and dismissed them. The jury cleared the courtroom.

Following the guilty verdicts, Judge Anderson moved immediately into the sentencing of Byron Smith.

Peter Orput asked the court to give Smith the maximum sentence allowed by the state of Minnesota: life in prison without the possibility of parole.

Orput said Smith should serve consecutive life sentences.

Orput told Judge Anderson, "Each body counts, each murder counts. In the end, it may be superfluous, but it's not for the families."

Judge Anderson denied Orput's request for consecutive sentences, saying it would not change the length of the ultimate sentence. He then sentenced Smith to life in prison without the possibility of parole.

After the verdict, family members of Brady and Kifer read victim-impact statements before the court.

On behalf of Kifer's parents, Kifer's aunt, Laurie Skipper, said Smith's actions were a conscious decision that took Kifer away from her family forever.

She said the day of the shootings was the worst day of their lives, and listening to the audio recording from inside Smith's home was unbearable.

"You always want to protect your children, and we weren't able to do that. The audio will forever haunt the family."

Nick Brady's mother, Kimberly Brady, described her son as kind, big-hearted, and eager to learn.

"Not seeing him anymore is a great tragedy, a tremendous sadness that never seems to go away."

Brady's grandmother, Bonnie Schaeffel, said Smith seemed like a sour, angry old recluse who felt he was above the law. She added she was sorry his house was burglarized but said, "Haile and Nick should have had consequences so they could learn from their mistakes. Mr. Smith took that away from them."

Smith was then given the chance to address the court. He declined.

Smith was remanded into custody immediately after court was adjourned. The court bailiff escorted Smith out of the courtroom and up the stairs to the jail.

The Morrison County Jail made preparations to transport Smith to the St. Cloud Prison within the following few days. From there, Smith would be sent to a maximum-security prison so he could spend the rest of his life behind bars.

POST-CONVICTION
NEWS COVERAGE

As people were exiting the courtroom, journalists were waiting in the hallway to get people's reactions.

Meshbesher told them, "There's a lot of things missing. To disregard those things is wrong . . . to get a fair trial without viewing all the evidence is extremely difficult and near impossible to do."

Meshbesher said he felt the verdict was a wrongful conviction, and he intended to take the case to the Minnesota Supreme Court.

I felt Meshbesher was sensationalizing the case to the media, because first-degree murder convictions are automatically reviewed by the Supreme Court anyway.

I also felt that some of Meshbesher's comments were disrespectful to the twelve jurors who had to endure the trial and make that very difficult decision. It's not like they chose to be on the jury. They were picked. Meshbesher's team picked some of them during the jury selection process.

Orput said, "I don't feel a sense of gloating. I just feel a sense of real sadness. We've got two dead kids, over nothing."

A conference room was set up in the courthouse and the news media all filed in. News cameras were lined up in a long row behind a podium. A post-conviction news conference was held. I went in to watch.

Our sheriff, Michel Wetzel, opened the news conference. He recalled telling the media that this case was not about a person's right to protect himself in his own home. "That's a given."

Wetzel said the case involved deciding where the limits were before and after a threat occured.

"In this case, a jury decided there are limits, and they've decided where they are. My office respects the process, and we respect the jury's verdict."

Brady's grandfather, Steve Schaeffel, represented the family in addressing the media.

Schaeffel said Smith took something from his family that can never be replaced. "These kids made a dumb mistake. I have made huge, stupid mistakes in my life, but I'm alive to talk about it. Justice was served today in the verdict."

Peter Orput told the press there were no winners in this case. Three people had lost their lives in this matter. "This wasn't a case about self-protection, but rather a senseless, sad, premeditated murder of two kids."

A couple jurors agreed to talk with the media after the trial.

The *Star Tribune* newspaper reported that juror Thomas Strandberg said, "For the most part, we were all pretty much in agreement from the start. We just wanted to make sure that we thought about all the evidence that was in front of us, and we wanted to go over everything that we had in front of us. Other than that, there wasn't a whole lot of sticking points, so to speak."

Juror Evelyn Mrosla agreed, saying one juror held out from agreeing to the guilty verdicts for a while, "but it just went fast, though."

Even the lone holdout wasn't arguing for acquittal, but "just wanted to be sure," said Strandberg.

Several other jurors declined to comment in detail, saying only that it was a tough case to hear but not a tough one to decide.

When the news conference was over, Peter and I went to our usual smoking spot for our final goodbyes.

"I'm glad we won the case for the victims' families' sake, but I sure don't feel any sense of celebrating the victory," I told Peter.

"I agree. It's just a sad case all around."

Peter gave me his business card and told me to keep in contact with him. He also invited me to come down to his office someday for a tour and to have lunch with him.

I thanked him for all his hard work in this case. I gave him my business card and told him to call me if he ever needed anything. We shook hands and went our separate ways.

CONCLUSION

I went home after work and told Chrissy the good news. The case was finally over, and we had won. She told me she was glad things were finally over and our life could get back to normal. I was hopeful for the same, but I was afraid things were probably far from over for some people.

We finished our painting project in our new home and moved in shortly after the trial ended. Jamie was reluctant to help me move, but he also understood our reasons.

A couple of weeks after the trial ended, *Dateline NBC* contacted our office and wanted to do a show about the Byron Smith case. Sheriff Wetzel told me they wanted to interview me for the show. I agreed to it, hoping the episode would help people to better understand what the case had really been about.

I called and talked with Peter Orput because I wanted his opinion about doing the show. He said *Dateline NBC* called him, too, and he also agreed to do it. We both hoped it would help people to understand that this case was not about taking people's legal rights away or taking their guns away. It was about one man who chose to do a very bad thing.

It was pretty exciting to be asked to be on a national news show. Not many officers or investigators do something like that in their careers.

As the weeks and months passed by, I stayed busy, even on my days off, trimming the oak trees in the new yard and doing other projects around the new house. The house didn't have a central air unit, so I paid to have a new one installed, for example.

The housing market was slow at that time and my old house hadn't sold yet. Instead of one lawn, I had two to mow.

Work had been crazy as usual, and there was no shortage of evening and late-night call outs for me to respond to.

I was hoping the harassment would end once the case was over, but it didn't. The Byron Smith coalition appeared to be working even harder, chasing Smith's appeal.

I started getting threatening phone calls at work from random people in other states. They were blaming me for arresting Smith, and holding me responsible for his conviction. Of course, these cowards refused to identify themselves when I asked them who I was speaking to.

I had done my job. My sworn duty was to the public. They payed me to do my job. I was the fact gatherer and had followed the rule of law set in place by the people.

I was not on the twelve-panel jury. I was not among those who ultimately convicted Smith for murder. I also was not the judge who sentenced Smith to life in prison without the possibility of parole. Yet, people blamed me.

Chrissy told me she was getting harassed at work just because she was married to me.

In August of 2014, four short months after the trial, while sitting in the living room one evening watching TV, Chrissy told me she had finally reached her breaking point.

She told me she wanted a divorce. She said she just couldn't live this way anymore. She said she had no idea being married to an investigator was going to be like this.

I was devastated. Chrissy was the love of my life, and we had a beautiful daughter together. Destroyed as I was, I didn't blame Chrissy. She knew being an investigator and helping people was my passion in life. She also knew I would never give it up. I told her I was sorry for everything she had to go through. I knew it was not fair and she should not have had to endure everything she had.

We sat on the front porch, had a cup of coffee, and talked peacefully about how we would separate. We agreed that Chrissy would keep the new house, and I would keep the old house.

The next day, I grabbed some of my belongings and moved back into my old house. I was glad it hadn't sold. I was back, living in the house that held ten years of my marriage memories.

By October 2014, our divorce was finalized. After ten years of marriage, I was single and lonely again.

Even today, as I sit in my living room, looking out the window at the squirrels chasing each other, one thought remains in my mind. Nick and Haile lost their lives. Byron lost his freedom. And I lost my family.

Born and raised in Little Falls, a central-Minnesota town of 8,300 people, Jeremy L. Luberts is a second-generation law enforcement officer who spent nearly three decades with the Morrison County Sheriff's Office. Jeremy was a patrol officer, then a sergeant investigator, eventually becoming lead investigator on the Byron Smith murder case. Now retired, Jeremy wants to share his knowledge of and experience with a case that will impact him for the rest of his life.

Jeremy continues to live in Little Falls, tucked among oak trees and farm fields.